Praise for *First-Time Dad*

First-Time Dad serves up first-rate advice.

—JIM DALY, president and CEO, Focus on the Family, and author of *Stronger*

More than thirty years ago I became a father, but I'll admit I was terrified about how to be a good dad to my little girl. My childhood was full of pain, and I had an acute sense of my own severe shortcomings and unpreparedness to be a father. If that's your story, too, you'll benefit from this great book. *First-Time Dad* is an easy read, full of practical advice, and I highly recommend it for new fathers.

—JOSH MCDOWELL, speaker and author of *The Father Connection*

I can't think of a better resource for new fathers than John Fuller's excellent new book, *First-Time Dad*. I write as one who has seen firsthand what happens when Dad isn't there. It's the lack of a male role model that has caused hundreds of thousands of young Americans to turn to the gangs and then end up in prison. I'm grateful to my friend John for producing such a tremendous resource.

—CHUCK COLSON, founder, Prison Fellowship and The Colson Center for Christian Worldview

Along with the diaper bag this book needs to put in the hands of every new dad. Through John's insight and experience he has managed to capture the seriousness and humor of being a dad and provide a biblical, heartfelt, and practical resource that will help serve to navigate the waters of fatherhood.

—PHIL JOEL, Christian recording artist and father of two

I remember leaving the hospital with our new baby—I desperately wanted them to give me an "instruction manual" that day—and while it's a little late for us, you're holding a must-read, practical, encouraging, biblical, humorous book if you're about to become a First-Time Dad!

—JOHN TRENT, PhD, president, StrongFamily, coauthor of *The Blessing*

When John Fuller speaks, I listen. In *First-Time Dad*, he speaks candidly with authority, focus, and direction. This is more than just another good book on being a dad; this should be required reading for every dad.

—DR. DENNIS RAINEY, host, FamilyLife Today

A child can throw a major league curveball on a man's life and his marriage. In *First-Time Dad*, John helps a new daddy understand what an awesome privilege it is to be a dad. Any new dad will feel encouraged, gain insight, and find great help, as they begin that wonderful, exciting journey of being a new dad!

—DR. KEVIN LEMAN, psychologist and author of *Have a New Kid by Friday*

Here are real-world tips from a six-time dad and a master communicator. Fun, memorable, useful. Guys, buy this book if you want to learn how to be more than merely the "masculine parental unit"— it'll teach you how to be what you've always wanted to be—an awesome Dad!

—FRANK PASTORE, talk show host, author of *Shattered*

John's the kind of dad who is always intentionally thinking about how to invest in the lives of his kids to make them better. *First-Time Dad* will help fathers understand what to expect when kids enter the family, how to continue loving their wives in the context of the family, and ultimately how to be a dad kids will look up to and respect. Thanks, John. We need this book!

—ANDY BRANER, international speaker, author, and full-time dad

In *First-Time Dad*, John's experience as a loving father of six will replace fear and trembling with hope and excitement for every dad who is wondering what he has gotten himself into. Tackling everything from looking after your new infant to impacting your teen, John's wise and thoughtful approach gives first-time dads—and every dad—a wide assortment of practical ideas for interacting with their kids, building lasting relationships, and making memories that they and their kids will treasure forever.

—TODD CARTMELL, child psychologist and author of *Project Dad* the stuff you really need to know

first-time dad

JOHN FULLER

Cohost of the Focus on the Family *Daily Broadcast*

WITH PAUL BATURA

JRR,

Just a little something
To maybe help with the
emmense task ahead!

Love Ya All
Jess & Phil

MOODY PUBLISHERS
CHICAGO

© 2011 by
JOHN FULLER

Edited by Andy Scheer
Interior design: Ragont Design
Cover design: Faceout Studios
Cover image: RF Shutterstock #27851134 and #49975618
Author Photo: Patti Watkins/Inspired Studios Photography

Library of Congress Cataloging-in-Publication Data

Fuller, John
    First-time dad : the stuff you really need to know / John Fuller, with
Paul Batura.
      p. cm.
    ISBN 978-0-8024-8750-6
    1. Fatherhood. 2. Fatherhood—Religious aspects—Christianity.
I. Batura, Paul J. II. Title.
HQ756.F85 2011
306.874'2—dc22
                                                         2011001271

We hope you enjoy this book from Moody Publishers. Our goal is to provide high-quality, thought-provoking books and products that connect truth to your real needs and challenges. For more information on other books and products written and produced from a biblical perspective, go to www. moodypublishers.com or write to:

Moody Publishers
820 N. LaSalle Boulevard
Chicago, IL 60610

1 3 5 7 9 10 8 6 4 2

Printed in the United States of America

This book is dedicated to Thomas L. Fuller, for modeling in word and deed how to be a good dad; to my six children, for the awesome privilege of being your dad—and the wonderful laughter we enjoy along the way; to my beloved wife, Dena, for your heart of gold, constant encouragement, faithfulness as a mom and wife, and patient love.

Contents

Chapter 1

Great Expectations

I am giddy; expectation whirls me round.
—WILLIAM SHAKESPEARE

FROM THE MOMENT you learned about the pregnancy (or that you were going to adopt), you've been anticipating that little one. This chapter will help you deal with your fears and expectations about your coming years as a dad—and offer practical suggestions for managing the many changes headed your way.

On a recent Saturday morning, I found myself facing a tedious chore. After too many years, it was time to weed out the files in our home office. I'm not sure what I expected to find, but in a matter of minutes, I found myself awash in wonderful memories.

My wife, Dena, had saved physician records going back twenty years, and am I glad she did. The documents tracked our struggle to become parents and recorded her numerous visits, early in our marriage, with the obstetrician-gynecologist. We were anxious to have kids, but conception eluded us time and again.

Our season of infertility spanned nearly two years. That's relatively brief compared to the anguish many couples face when trying to conceive, but it was still a painful season for us. At the time, it consumed us. But now, two decades and six children later, I realized how the years had softened the memories of that emotional time. I had forgotten the difficulties and disappointments, the months of tears and sorrow as we faced another door closing on our hopes to become parents.

My mind wandered back as I read the doctor's notes, and I smiled as I remembered that day when, after years of waiting, we finally had a positive pregnancy test! It was almost unbelievable. Really? Yes, the test is positive! What joy—we were (finally!) going to be parents!

Now What?

As the news began to sink in, our heads began to swirl. We knew we were headed for changes. Big changes! But we didn't know what those changes might be—or how we would weather them. We knew just enough to know that you don't know what you don't know.

On the positive side, we were confident we had a strong marriage and that this next stage of life—parenting—was something we were ready to experience. Despite our many questions, we expected it would be a pretty easy progression—a transition we believed we were prepared to handle and succeed at. Those expectations would soon meet reality.

For the next six or seven months, much of what we did together and talked about was centered on the "Little Fuller" we'd be welcoming into the world. We were excited! All was right with our world—or at least there was nothing wrong that our new child couldn't make right.

Little did we know that in only a few months we'd be stretched so tight and worn so thin we'd feel as if we would break. I could never have imagined we'd be arguing over the baby—and all kinds of things that now seem silly. I couldn't know how little sleep I'd learn to operate on. There was no way to prepare for the doubts and insecurities I would feel as a new dad. But fatigue, as Abraham Lincoln said, makes cowards of men.

But wait! We were in love. We got along famously! How could a baby pull us apart? And parenting—it can't be *that* hard; what's there to know? The answers to those questions are the inspiration for this book. It's never easy being a father—it's even more difficult being a first-time father. And keeping your marriage strong while you learn, on the job, takes a lot of effort.

Looking back over those old medical records, I came to a stark realization. Although I didn't know it at the time, I was sitting on a fault line, oblivious to the seismic changes coming our way.

Immediate Adjustments

Some of the changes we made prior to our child's birth seemed insignificant. Our conversations changed from "the two of us" to "the three of us." We started thinking about the car—it was a small hatchback—and wondered where we'd put the car seat and the stroller. We started thinking about the house and yard. The baby's room would need some paint and preparation, and the backyard wasn't adequately fenced—would we be comfortable letting the baby play back there?

Clearly "the baby" would need a lot of stuff. A bassinet, clothing, a stroller, car seat, diapers, etc. We had a lot of shopping to do. We reveled in discussing the "best" things to get and enjoyed visiting stores trying to find great deals. Of course, new things meant we had to rearrange our house to make room. The spare bedroom in our modest house became the nursery. Painting and cleaning together, we prepared to become first-time parents.

Thoughts about what life would be like with "Junior" occupied our minds and our conversations. What would he or she (we didn't know the baby's gender) be like? What name would we choose? Would she have Dena's brunette hair or my blond locks? What would we have to do to meet his needs? How would we help her to be happy and to eventually grow into the adult God intended? We sifted through a variety of expectations about children and about being parents.

We started reading pregnancy books that showed the baby's growth and the ongoing effects on Mom's body. We took "husband-coached childbirth" classes so we could welcome this baby into the world in the best manner possible. We checked out baby name books and parenting books from the library. We listened to radio programs like *Focus on the Family* to learn about parenthood concerns. We talked and spent time with experienced parents. We tried our best to prepare for the new responsibility we'd undertake in a few months. We knew there was a lot we *didn't* know, so we endeavored to learn as much as possible.

Ready! Ready!

If you visit the Amtrak level of New York City's Penn Station, you'll notice a large schedule board that hangs from the ceiling. At rush hour, crowds gather there, sometimes several people deep, to await their train's track assignment. People are eager to make a beeline for the train to get a good seat. Just prior to the boarding announcement, a voice bellows from the speakers: "Ready! Ready! Ready! Ready!" The passengers grab their bags and brace themselves for the sprint downstairs.

That's a lot how we felt in those days leading up to Dakota's arrival. We were ready. Our bags were packed, and we had one in each hand. If having a child is akin to a college final, we were prepared to ace the exam. Within months we were set to take on the biggest responsibility we'd ever known, the most significant work a person can do. We knew that raising a child is a fearful and wonderful job, one that never really ends, but one for which we were as prepared as we could be.

Or so we thought.

Simply thinking, reading, and talking about our new roles of dad and mom wasn't enough. Looking back, I realize just how little I really knew about being a dad when our firstborn entered the world.

Once Dakota arrived we found ourselves feeling confident and capable one day—then perplexed and overwhelmed the next. There were times we screamed in frustration or cried with sorrow about our inability to meet this child's needs. There were moments we wondered how we'd make it through another sleepless night. (That's when I discovered coffee!) There would be long evenings at home when we wished we could find or afford a babysitter for even a few hours respite from this child's demands. Why didn't he sleep? He needed around-the-clock care, and I constantly found myself fumbling my responsibilities.

Isn't this baby thing supposed to be natural and intuitive? Can't we just figure this out?

What should I have done differently? What might have helped me—and our newly expanded family—more than buying baby gear, reading about the birthing process, and having a plan for taking off work those first few days? What had I missed?

For starters, it would have helped to understand my expectations.

Great Expectations

Let's get honest. What do you expect about parenting? What will family life be like for you? How will a baby affect your marriage? What will fatherhood do for—and to—you? Will you find fulfillment? Excitement? Satisfaction? Closure? Will your child bring out the best in you? Do you fear how you might react to parenting challenges because your own childhood wasn't pretty? What do you think fatherhood will be all about?

These are important questions because your expectations affect your parenting style, your interactions with your child and your wife, and your self-assessments about your effectiveness as a dad.

Do you expect parenting to come naturally and be easy? Do you think having a child will present exciting new challenges that will bring fulfillment and satisfaction? Do you think you'll have days of frustration and exhaustion? Is the opportunity to shape a little life exhilarating? Will you wonder if you will be a good dad or if you will totally blow it?

Well, the answers to all of the above are likely to be "Yes"!

Reviewing my journal entries early in my parenting journey, I had wonderful and well-meaning expectations. I also experienced plenty of differing emotions. There were joyous times early on, and as our son grew there were also some pretty trying times. We delighted in being a mom and dad, but occasionally we asked what in the world we'd gotten ourselves into. Some days being a father seemed perfectly natural, and other days I'd scratch my head and wonder what I was supposed to do next. At times we *loved* having a little one to care for, at other times we longed for the good old days.

Time has taught me one of the most important things is this: The emotional roller coaster I found myself on was perfectly normal. You can expect to have alternating joy and heartache as you raise your child. That *will* happen. You'll most likely have many great days as a dad, when you feel that you really know what you are doing and that you are successful as a father. You'll also have days when you'll wonder how—or even if—you can go on. There will be days you'll think you've totally failed. Every father has his moments of glory, as well as his moments of doubt.

The Time Machine

Let's look at a historical figure—one who had plenty of expectations because he had to wait for years to become a dad. In the first book of the Bible, we see that Abraham and his wife, Sarah, had a long, fruitful life—but no children together. That changed when an angel announced that, despite their advanced years, things were going to change—drastically!

Sarah, who was in her nineties, laughed at the angel's announcement that she would give birth within a year. Abraham reacted similarly, but you can be sure he was pondering the news, remembering God's promise that he'd have many descendants. After years of waiting, and being past the age of having kids, Abe (who was one hundred years old) had to be wondering what was happening—and what would happen in the coming months.

As the days approached, Abraham must have run through the disappointments of the past years as he waited for God to deliver on His promise. When first pondering his future as a father, did Abraham think about the joy of raising a child, playing hide-and-seek, telling stories, perhaps hunting together, and maybe even envision the practical benefits of children in that culture (like taking care of the parents in their old age)?

Now a century old, Abraham must also have thought this to be an impossible fulfillment to his decades of dreaming. And what about the timing? I can hear him talking with the Creator. "God, how could You wait so long? You are aware of my age, aren't You?"

Here's a man who has waited decades to share parenthood with his wife. During that time he surely anticipated what life would be like when Sarah finally delivered their first child. Now he'd be a hundred years old and raising a newborn! Talk about unfulfilled dreams. At Abraham's age, how could he possibly protect—or play with—his long-awaited child?

The Serenity of Sovereignty

At the risk of serving up a cliché, the sooner we accept that God's ways are not always our wishes, the better off we'll be. As we can see from Abraham's example, dads have long had problems with unrealistic and unmet expectations about fatherhood. In the process of dealing with those expectations, we dads often make mistakes and have to face a lot of failings. What's a new dad to do?

First, take heart: Children are very forgetful—and also very forgiving. Although I made every possible mistake, and feared for years that I had permanently scarred him, my oldest son recently told me he thinks I've been a good dad. This was a pleasant surprise! It was also a wonderful gift from God to let me know I had not done as poor a job at fathering as I had felt.

Despite my shortcomings, my oldest, on whom I had practiced all my first-time dad experiments, felt loved enough to affirm *me*. What joy (and relief)!

Tackling Fears

Each of us brings baggage to our parenting. It's inevitable. But you have a choice: You don't have to hold on to that baggage.

If your own childhood was picture-perfect and wonderfully memorable, you'll probably enter into parenthood with optimistic expectations that you'll be a fine dad and that raising a child will be easy. If you'd rather put your childhood memories far, far away, you'll likely doubt your ability as a parent. You also might be anxious about parenting because of fears you'll duplicate your parents' mistakes.

If there's one man who should have feared being a dad, it would be my friend Jim Daly, whose father left the family when Jim was five. After a couple of years in which Jim lacked an adult male figure in his life, Jim's mom married a man who was hostile toward her five kids. The day of his mom's funeral (she died from cancer when Jim was nine), that stepfather walked out of the home and left the children to fend for themselves. In a few short years, Jim had experienced terrible modeling by those two men. His biological dad showed selfishness and a lack of accountability to his family. His stepdad repeated that example.

When Jim became a man, who could have blamed him for fearing he'd repeat those patterns of parenting?

The good news is that, with God's help, Jim Daly is a fine father to two young boys. He makes time for them, he loves them in ways they can appreciate, and he loves their mom and models a wonderful Christian marriage to his kids. While quick to admit he isn't perfect, Jim is breaking the chain of bad living and making a huge difference in the lives of his wife and children. He shows that a new family tree can be planted, and that fear doesn't have to prevent a man from becoming a good dad.

Practical Advice

How can you properly approach the role of dad? Here are some ideas to consider:

1. Read quality books and watch videos about parenting. There are dozens of good resources from well-regarded experts, and I'll refer to many of my favorites throughout *First-Time Dad*. Take advantage of the seasoned, wise advice of others.

2. Spend time with experienced parents. Watch them. Watch their kids. Make mental notes. Write things down. Launch conversations from their experiences with their kids. Find a mentor couple to walk you through the coming days, someone to offer experienced perspectives to help you as a new dad.

3. Discuss with your spouse your hopes, fears, and expectations about being a new parent. Talk about your pasts. Address your expectations about how you will approach this monumental task. Make sure that, where you have differences, you've talked those through and come to a shared understanding of areas of common ground you can agree on.

4. Pray about your new parental responsibilities. Ask God to help you be the dad your child needs, and to supply what you lack.

5. Journal about the road ahead. This is something a lot of men struggle with, as such thinking can lead to . . . feelings. And many men run from emotions. But consider taking the time, even if you are very busy, to think things through to deep levels—and to record those reflections on your computer or in a journal. It can help to express your thoughts and feelings— in real time, as you encounter various situations.

Now that we've addressed your expectations, let's turn our attention to a critical question: *If our dreams and ideals of fatherhood are often shaded by unrealistic expectations, what is fatherhood really all about?*

Ten Friendly Warnings

Some friendly warnings I share with you about your coming years as a dad:

1. Never think you've blown it so badly that your child will be adversely affected forever. Kids are resilient. I'm not suggesting you ignore your mistakes, just keep things in perspective.

2. Don't forget your wife probably has a great handle on what your child needs. Trust her intuition.

3. Don't think these days are forever. They only feel that way. One day soon you'll wake up and wonder how this baby got to be nine years old. Enjoy today. Drink it in. Be grateful for all of it.

4. Don't become so caught up in surviving these early years that you forget to keep the end in mind. Your goal as a dad is to help your daughter become an adult—and then step out of the way. This realization becomes especially important as your child enters the toddler years; your wife will need some long-term perspective and hope.

5. Don't yield to the temptation to escape the challenges of home by taking up a time-consuming hobby or becoming a workaholic. Right now, and for the next eighteen or so years, your child and your wife need you. Put them first . . . you'll have time later to indulge in that hobby.

6. Don't believe the lie that kids just need "quality time" and that you can delay investing in your son's life until he's older. Build into that child every day. Let me repeat: every day.

7. Don't miss the milestones. If I could do it over again, I'd bring home ice cream more often and do more to celebrate my children's accomplishments and special occasions.

8. Don't be impatient with your child. It's a common mistake to expect more than is age-appropriate, especially from a firstborn. Have patience, Dad, in her ability to understand and to behave.

9. Don't let this baby define you. Some guys pin their entire existence and self-worth on how they perform as a dad. Bad idea. You'll mess up a lot and you'll constantly feel inadequate. Why ruin your self-esteem by making "dad" your only role in life? Besides, while you are now a dad, you are also still many other things: a husband, an employee (or employer), a son, a brother . . .

10. Don't think you can accomplish this fatherhood thing alone. I've learned a lot from other dads. I've tried to be a student of other men, seeing how they handle certain ages and challenges. I've belonged to several small groups where we could share common frustrations and joys about being a dad. I've read lots of books about being a good father. And I've tried to incorporate something helpful into my life from everything I've learned.

Chapter 2

What Fatherhood Is All About

One father is more than a hundred schoolmasters.

—GEORGE HERBERT

IF YOU REMEMBER only one thing from this chapter, I pray you'll remember this: *Don't take your cues about fatherhood from the culture, but rather from the God of the universe.*

Truett Cathy is probably best known for his Chick-fil-A restaurants, and while I like the food he helped make popular, I'm most appreciative of the work he does to help boys who face the prospect of growing up without a father.

Mr. Cathy has been mentoring youngsters for more than sixty years. He runs a camp and foster-care program designed to help give children of broken homes a second chance at life. It's an inspiring program. Boys are matched with mentors and father figures, and some are even placed in full-time Christian foster homes. Many are given the opportunity to work side by side with Mr. Cathy on a beautiful farm in the rolling hills of Rome, Georgia.

Truett Cathy is a well-seasoned Southern gentleman. But he's more than a nice guy with business savvy. He knows how boys think. Most important, he knows what they need: a father or—at the very least—a strong male role model. Mr. Cathy travels the country with a simple but strong message: You can make a difference! It's better to build boys than to have to mend men.

In many ways, that's the journey you're embarking on as a first-time dad. You're preparing to build your son or daughter, a monumental task given today's prevailing forces.

Bad Examples

Depictions of fatherhood in popular culture have come a long and sorry way. There was a time when the media suggested that a father knew best and had a firm grasp on the complexities of his kids. Bill Cosby's character of Dr. Cliff Huxtable clearly loved his kids, and the show did a great job depicting a normal family struggling to live a normal life.

But that era has passed. *Denver Post* editorial page editor Dan Haley recently noted that 2010 saw the passing of "two iconic

TV parents. . . . Barbara Billingsley, who played the perfect, sub-urban mom, June Cleaver, on *Leave It to Beaver*, and Tom Bosley, who most famously portrayed Howard Cunningham, the com-passionate patriarch of the *Happy Days* clan."

"They were relics of a time when television tried to por-tray perfection," Haley wrote in the November 28, 2010, *Denver Post*. "While the imagery of the idealized . . . nuclear family sitting down to enjoy an evening dinner together wasn't always realistic, the concept was valued in our culture and it was the goal."

Sitcom fathering has slipped in recent years. Dysfunctional depictions of fatherhood might get laughs, but they don't serve up redeeming examples of parenting. When Homer Simpson tells his son that alcohol is "the cause of and solution to all of life's problems," what's a guy to think?

It seems the news media also offer little positive coverage of fathers. Rarely do we read about a dad who is responsible, does the best he can for his wife and kids, and lives life well.

Unfortunately, it's the noise that tends to make news. We read about when a man makes a terrible choice and abuses his child, or perhaps when a celebrity says something awful about his father, but we don't see many positive references about fathers. Celebrity dads dominate the headlines, and often those men show a lack of commitment to their kids. They leave when life gets uncomfortable or when there's another, more exciting woman to pursue.

Cause for Pause

At this stage, the prospect of abandoning your new child is unfathomable. Sadly, the facts across America tell a very different story. The United States is the world's leader in father-less homes. The impact is breathtaking: 63 percent of youth suicides come from fatherless homes, and 75 percent of all adolescent patients in drug treatment centers come from homes without a dad. In his book *It's Better to Build Boys than Mend Men*, Truett Cathy offers these startling statistics:[1]

Children from fatherless homes are:

- 5 times more likely to commit suicide.
- 32 times more likely to run away.
- 20 times more likely to have behavioral disorders.
- 14 times more likely to commit rape.
- 9 times more likely to drop out of school.
- 10 times more likely to abuse chemical substances.
- 9 times more likely to end up in a state-operated institution.
- 20 times more likely to end up in prison.

Such revelations should drive every wayward father home and cause every dad teetering on divorce to do whatever he can to salvage the marriage.

The good news is that as a first-time father, by even picking up this book, you're making an investment to protect you and your family against future trouble. But just reading a book won't be enough to protect you from making one of the worst mistakes of your life.

The Father Is the Leader of the Band

The late Dr. Adrian Rogers was senior pastor of Bellevue Baptist Church and the founder of Love Worth Finding Ministries. He was also a longtime board member of Focus on the Family, and I count myself privileged to have crossed paths with this great saint. Dr. Rogers often referred to a father as "the leader of the band" whose home could be a symphony of praise, assuming he properly orchestrated the beautiful music found in a happy home. Dr. Rogers was right.

When it came to the importance of fatherhood, Dr. Rogers didn't mince words. "A good dad fears God and as a result, he shows it by the way that he lives," he once wrote. "There is nothing more important than a man's integrity. Let me ask the fathers reading this: What do you want to be remembered for? The job you held? The yard you kept? The money you earned? I want my children to remember me for my character. I want them to say, 'My dad feared God. My dad walked in the ways of God.'"

Dr. Rogers suggested that a father should be judged by the character he lives, the contentment he learns, and the companion he loves. "It is difficult to be a good man, even more difficult to be a good husband," he said. "But most difficult (and most important) of all, is to be a good dad."

The Power of an Engaged Dad

Nick Collison was only eight when he inadvertently learned some valuable lessons about how to play basketball. Those crucial lessons were administered when Dave Collison, Nick's father, came home from coaching Iowa Falls High School and lamented how terrible their practice had been.

Nothing had gone right. From the player who couldn't pass on the three-on-one fast break to the player who didn't dive for a loose ball to the player who failed to work around a pick on defense. Whatever irritated Coach Collison, he mentioned it in the same frustrated way a teacher speaks of students who were nuisances in class. Young Nick listened and learned.

"He would talk about guys being lazy and selfish," Nick Collison says. "You pick up on that and you pick up on what you don't want to be as a player. . . . You grow to despise those kids, too. I was the manager or the ball boy, and I was getting on those kids."

Collison is now a veteran professional in the National Basketball Association. He is perhaps best known for his superior performances while playing college ball for the Kansas Jayhawks, where he was a career scoring and rebounding leader in the Big 12 Conference. But before the University of Kansas, Collison played for his father at Iowa Falls High School, where they had a phenomenal run, going 101-1 and winning two state titles. As a father and son, the Collisons won their last 52 games, quite an achievement for a school in a town of 5,500.

Nick absorbed his father's lessons for years before ever playing for him. "The things I picked up most was about being a good teammate," Nick said, "stepping up and playing well when you need it, but also being unselfish and being successful through your teammates."

The Climb to the Top

In Colorado, where our family makes its home, there are fifty-four "14ers" (mountains 14,000 feet or higher). Some outdoor enthusiasts make it a goal to climb all fifty-four. I recently heard about one man who was climbing Mount Princeton with his son. As they neared the summit and the father scanned the trail, the boy shouted out from behind, "Choose the good path, Dad; I'm coming right behind you!"

That little fellow was instinctively reminding his dad to live the words of Proverbs 22:6: "Train up a child in the way he should go; even when he is old he will not depart from it" (ESV). Or consider the apostle Paul's blunt admonition to the members of the church at Ephesus: "Fathers," he said, "do not provoke your children to anger, but bring them up in the discipline and instruction of the Lord" (Ephesians 6:4 ESV). Isn't that the whole point? You don't want to be a good father just for the sake of being a good father. You want to be a good father because you want to teach your son how to be a good man!

The Essence of Fathering

Our first-time dad adventure is just getting started, but before moving to our next area of focus, I'd like to share a few words from the late radio legend Paul Harvey. He and his wife had just one son, Paul Junior. Shortly after Paul Jr. turned five, Mr. Harvey reflected on his role as a dad. Here is what he wrote. I think it will resonate with you as much it did with me:

Who Is a Father?

A father is a person who is forced to endure childbirth without an anesthetic. He growls when he feels good and laughs very loud when he is scared half-to-death.

A father never feels entirely worthy of the worship in a child's eyes. He is never quite the hero his daughter thinks. Never quite the man his son believes him to be. And this worries him sometimes. (So he works too hard to try to smooth the rough places in the road of those of his own who will follow him.)

A father is a person who goes to war sometimes . . . and would run the other way except that war is part of an important job in his life (which is making the world better for his child than it has been for him).

Fathers grow older faster than other people, because they, in other wars, have to stand at the train station and wave goodbye to the uniform that climbs on board.

And, while mothers cry where it shows, fathers
stand and beam . . . outside . . . and die inside.

Fathers are men who give daughters away to other men
who aren't nearly good enough, so that they can have
children that are smarter than anybody's.

Fathers fight dragons almost daily. They hurry away from
the breakfast table off to the arena, which is sometimes
called an office or a workshop. There they tackle the
dragon with three heads: Weariness, Works, and Monotony.
And they never quite win the fight, but they never give up.

Knights in shining armor; fathers in shiny trousers. There's
little difference as they march away each workday.

And when Father passes away, and after a good rest, he won't
just sit on a cloud and wait for the girl he's loved and the children she bore. He'll be busy there too . . . repairing the stars,
oiling the gates, improving the streets, smoothing the way.

Suggested Resources

Complete Book of Baby & Child Care, by Paul C. Reisser,
M.D. (Focus on the Family).

Rattled: Surviving Your Baby's First Year, by Trish Berg
(Multnomah Publishers).

Straight Talk to Men, by James C. Dobson, Ph.D.
(Tyndale House).

*Eat, Sleep, Poop: A Common Sense Guide to Your Baby's
First Year,* by Scott W. Cohen, M.D. (Scribner).

Websites:

National Center for Fathering: www.fathers.com

National Fatherhood Initiative: www.fatherhood.org

Focus on the Family: www.focusonthefamily.com/
    parenting

Chapter 3

Time and Priorities

Time is what we want most,
but what . . . we use worst.
—WILLIAM PENN

NO MORE LEISURELY Saturdays! Brace yourself: A lot
of your time is about to be taken by that baby. But
wait—you've got so much to do around the house and
need that promotion to help pay the bills. This chapter
shows you why you should avoid spending too much
time at the office, on the road, or pursuing hobbies.

For me, one of the most appealing aspects of being newly married was the spontaneity Dena and I enjoyed as a couple. If we wanted to head off for a bike ride after church, we did. If we'd rather spend a quiet weekend afternoon, take a nap, or watch a movie, we'd ignore the phone and relax. If someone extended an invitation to dinner, we'd accept and not worry about what time we'd get home. Life was fairly unpredictable—and we liked it that way. The ability to flex our schedule was something we appreciated and valued.

Enter the baby.

A Dose of Reality

Even before Dakota was born, our first child affected our ability to be spontaneous. As the pregnancy progressed, my wife became less energetic and slept more as she turned her attentions to his due date. We both found ourselves doing more and more to prepare for his arrival. In our spare time, we readied his room. We painted, cleaned, and organized. Increasingly we stayed at home. I guess that nesting instinct was taking over. The slow evenings of reading, taking walks, talking . . . all that "do what we want when we want" began to fade.

At this stage, I know what some of you are thinking. *This parenting thing doesn't sound very attractive. Although I wouldn't consider myself selfish, I do enjoy my freedom. What you're describing sounds neither romantic nor fun. I signed up to be a father—not an indentured servant!*

A colleague remembers phoning a college friend some time ago to congratulate him on the arrival of their first child. After four rings he received the family's voice mail and heard this message:

Hi, you've reached the Gerrard family. I'm sorry we missed your call. I'm surprised you didn't find us at home. After all, we have no life. We have a baby. In fact, we're probably passed out from exhaustion. If we don't call you back within a short while, please call 911. We might very well be dead. Okay, I'm kidding. We're not dead. But it's true we have no life! Good-bye. Thanks for calling.

Funny—but what an attitude! Before addressing this type of cynicism, which seems too common, I'd like to share a brief story for context. I have a good friend who once served the president of the United States in a high-level capacity. He had access to the Oval Office and was regularly called on to offer the president advice on highly sensitive matters. I once asked him about the experience of serving up counsel that might not be warmly embraced. Here was his response:

"I was paid for my informed opinion," he said. "The very best way I could serve the president was not to tell him what he wanted to hear or what I wished the answer to be. Absolutely not! I served the president most faithfully when I gave it to him straight, laid it on the line, when I told him the way it really was."

As I offer advice for first-time fathers, I resonate with my friend's perspective. It's not my intent to paint a dreary picture of parenthood. Yet I don't want to offer up a shortsighted prescription that will not only frustrate but possibly do more harm than good.

As a happy father of six who is now in his twenty-second year of parenting, I believe this dilemma—the challenge of retaining our personal freedom while meeting parental responsibilities—is simply a matter of balancing our time and priorities. It's also the key to being a healthy and responsible husband and father.

What Not to Do

There are many things you can do as a dad when a baby arrives. Unfortunately, many men want to escape. They aren't comfortable with their parenting abilities—or they don't like the changes the baby brings. Or maybe they object to the new status in the home, coming in second or third behind little Junior and the family dog for the attentions of his wife.

I've seen guys do strange things to escape the chaotic home front. They might join four different soccer leagues. They start remodeling projects. Some guys take up bizarre new activities.

About that last item, it's confession time. About the time of our first child, I took up an extracurricular activity. I suddenly had a hankering to attend graduate school. During those first years after Dakota was born, school occupied a lot of my time. In my defense, this was something my wife and I had discussed for some time, and in many ways it was a labor of love intended to position me for a different job. But in hindsight, the timing was awful. With a new baby, my wife needed me home more—not less. But for about two years I commuted 250 miles, twice a week, to work on a graduate degree. Finally, circumstances changed and I had to abandon that pursuit.

Was I seeking an escape from my responsibilities as a new dad? Not intentionally. But I wish someone had told me about the importance of being more involved in my child's life, especially in those early years. Old family photos and videos show I was there for Dena and Dakota—just not as much as I now wish.

Lest you think that setting the right priorities is easy to master, a few years later I once again found myself back in grad school, pursuing that degree. This time, we had *four* children. While the stress of that commitment damaged our marriage, it also took a bit of a toll on our children. In many ways I was an absent dad. And I worked for a global family ministry!

After I finally got my master's degree, I determined not to repeat that mistake of doing too much outside the home. But for a couple of reasons, not the least of which were the continual promptings of a coworker and friend (along with my looming fortieth birthday), I found a passion for long-distance running. Running took hold of me.

As I prepared for my first marathon, my patient wife suggested I was spending a lot of time away from the family. She expressed doubts about my motives for taking an eighteen-mile run on a Saturday morning. Despite my assurances that the benefits of running were numerous and that my improved health was something to be thankful for, she remained skeptical. Dena's lack of appreciation made for some strained conversations. But I remained committed, so I pressed on with the training and races. And I hate to admit it, but my children had to move toward the back of the bus in my life.

If I knew then what I know now, I might have adjusted several of those early priorities. There's nothing inherently wrong with education or athletics. But as I chased those challenges, I was out of balance. I spent an inordinate amount of time away from home—and the wife and children I loved so dearly. It took some time for me to realize I'd have opportunities later in life, when the kids were older, to pursue those passions. The time I invested in stretching my mind and pushing my body, while worthy endeavors, did nothing to strengthen my family relationships. Those outside interests didn't say "I love you" to my children. In retrospect, I should have deferred graduate school for several years and been more of a weekend warrior in my running. I was out of balance—and nothing I do now can make up to Dena and the kids for those times I was away.

Work

For most first-time dads, the task of balancing work outside the home poses the greatest challenge. For a man in his twenties who wants to excel at work, it's easy to put in extra hours. The promotion path is clear. To get ahead means hard work during the early years on a job. "Doing the minimum" will pretty much guarantee being stuck in an entry-level position. And if that new dad is starting a business, the demands of getting things running require a lot of his time. Paradoxically, just when he should be turning his attentions to home, there is pressure to perform in the world of work. If a new dad isn't careful, he'll find himself pouring most of his energies into the paycheck.

Dad can probably get away with those additional at-work hours—if the new mom has turned her attention to the baby. She probably won't object if her husband stays late at the office every now and again. She's got her hands full and she's preoccupied by this precious new life. She might even think there's every good reason for him to be at the job more. With the arrival of Junior, the demands on the home budget are increasing. There's the need for a bigger place to live, mounting medical and grocery bills, and more. The financial needs of the growing family will only increase. Dad might as well work hard to get the promotion, or at the least, that pay raise.

So what can a man do? It's a pretty simple answer: Do less. Adjust your target, lower your sights, and do so for the right reasons: your dear wife and precious child.

The key to managing this balancing act is to reexamine your motives. Are you really working to get ahead—or might you be trying to escape the new demands of home? Check your motives. Only you can answer these questions. You've got to confront them.

As you wrestle with the "why" of your pursuits, maybe you'll realize that settling for less in some areas so you can build a strong relational bond with your child is really an excellent trade-off. This isn't compromising. This is a rational way to go after what Steven Covey calls a win-win. Decide to be content with a bit less prestige and a lot more satisfaction as a dad (and husband) and you'll be the envy of a lot of guys. I've known some driven men who, when they recognized how much of their life had been about work—and not about being husband and dad—made drastic course corrections. Not one told me he was sorry he took that pay cut or transferred to a less-consuming job. To a man, they indicated they're so glad they chose to seek balance where there had previously been none.

Real Life

I recall one coworker who usually stayed at work for hours past quitting time. At first I admired his dedication, and felt a bit guilty because I went home before he did almost every evening. I'd stay late occasionally, but this guy was a Superman. Despite his extreme hours, I never understood just what he did that was so important. Eventually, I realized he had three little children at home, and while he loved them, he probably found more fulfillment at work than at home. The office was easier to deal with than those unpredictable, complex children. For many men, it seems easier to work within the structure of the job than to try to navigate the complex nuances of parenting.

Compared to times at home and being a dad, most jobs provide guys with a sense of accomplishment. At work there's usually some kind of checklist, even if it's only cleaning up the in-box or making important phone calls. Or the concrete got poured. Or the sale was completed. We're usually given opportunities to measure our output and to have some feelings of

being competent. Thus it is pretty easy to be there—a lot—
mentally and physically.

But spending too much time at your job will rob your
child of time you can never make up.

Arthur Gordon, a former editor and bestselling author,
once recalled a cherished memory of childhood:

> When I was around thirteen and my brother ten, Father
> had promised to take us to the circus. But at lunchtime
> there was a phone call; some urgent business required his
> attention downtown. We braced ourselves for the disap-
> pointment. Then we heard him say, "No, I won't be down.
> It'll have to wait."
>
> When he came back to the table, Mother smiled. "The
> circus keeps coming back, you know."
>
> "I know," said Father. "But childhood doesn't."

Sixty years later, Arthur Gordon still remembered that
moment. In the days to come, I hope you will as well when it
comes to making decisions related to family and work.

Tough Truth

I wonder if you can identify with this truth: Men tend to
gravitate toward success and run from failure. While we may
not have great success at work, at least we know that we got
something done in a given day.

Not so with parenting! Sure, some duties are easily completed, allowing for a sense of competence and fulfillment.
But the chores of diapers and feedings are soon eclipsed by
other important needs like character development and helping your child understand the world. How can I put those
into a checklist? Let's see, taught my baby about gravity . . .

check? Or played peek-a-boo today and earned my parenting stripes? The task of parenting is a lifelong assignment. As a new dad you've only begun the journey of raising, training, and ultimately releasing a child into the world.

There's no way to feel you've completed the daddy task . . . at least not for two or three decades. Someone once suggested, "You don't know how you've done as a parent until your kids are raising your grandkids." There's no short-term, measurable way to gauge your effectiveness as a parent until . . . a long time from now! I'm not yet a grandparent. While from all indications my children are doing pretty well, I still have plenty of fathering challenges—and lingering doubts about how I am doing as a dad. So you'll probably be waiting a long time to determine how that daddy thing has been going.

Because you have to persevere on the home front for a long time, it's important to accept your doubts. As a dad, you get no annual reviews, few "attaboys," and little immediate feedback. So you'll need to persevere and settle in for the long haul.

Engage with Your Child

There are many ways you can invest in your child's life. Doing so doesn't require a special degree or even a lot of money or creativity. Some of the best ways to make special times with your child occur naturally in the rhythms of life, the everyday ebb and flow.

Here are a few examples.

Bedtime Routines

Bedtime is a special time to be with your child. Try to hold, read to, and cuddle with your baby every night. Mom will thank you (she'll welcome a break from the day's work!) and you'll build a stronger father-child bond.

Almost every night it's my job to handle the bedtime routine for our youngest, who is now in first grade. We might play awhile, and then it's off to brush his teeth and get his pajamas on. Then we read a couple books, maybe even three. I'll tuck him into bed, give him his drink of water, put my hand on his head, and pray for him. Then it's lights off, a final "I love you," and I know he's settled in with the assurance that I love him and like to spend time with him. This little ritual varies from time to time, but more often than not it's what we do each evening.

Mom loves to see me interacting with and loving on that little guy. She'll often smile and later may tell me how much she loves watching me be dad to her kids. Such affirmations mean a lot.

Errands

Never make a trip to the hardware store without your child. Well, sometimes that isn't the smartest move, but as your son or daughter gets older, bring them along as you run errands! That informal time together will be priceless.

I remember when our first child was about three. As I worked on various home projects, I'd make two or three trips to the hardware store. He'd jump into the back where his car seat was—and off we'd go. Along the way I'd chat about the sights (Look at that police car! How many red cars do you see?), we'd listen to music (appropriate for little ears), and we'd discuss where we were going and what I'd be buying. This seems pretty simple, right? It is!

Home Improvement

If you are doing some home improvement project, let your child stay at your side. There will be times when you are operating a saw or some power tool that isn't safe for Junior to be around (use common sense). But there's a lot even a two- or three-year-old can learn by watching you.

When he was about three, Dakota was by my side as I changed some interior door handles. A few days later, he had my toolbox in hand (since it was heavy, he dragged it along). He announced he was going to "fix the door." We chuckled, and didn't think twice about it . . . until we heard a clanging and realized he had just removed the bathroom doorknob! To this day he remains curious and mechanically inclined, and I'd like to think that some of that came from our times working around the house.

Mealtime

Feeding your child might seem mundane, but make a point of doing this whenever you can. You'll have an opportunity to be up close with your baby, and you'll be able to observe her growth and influence her cognitive and emotional development when you interact this way.

Daddy Time

It may seem weird, but as your child gets to the toddler stage, take him or her out on a date from time to time. Make it fun, but recognize this doesn't have to be an expensive outing.

- Visit the mall—many have kids' play areas.
- Go to the toy store to look around.
- Make your way to a local park and push the swing.
- Load 'em up in the bicycle trailer and go for a ride.
- Take a walk around the neighborhood. Visit the Y for swim lessons.

I've done all these things and found them easy, inexpensive, and priceless for making memories and having special one-on-one daddy time with each of my six children.

I've tried to outline for you that:

1. It is natural for you to want to escape from the unfamiliar, overwhelming responsibility of being a new dad.
2. Among other distractions, work will gladly pull you away from the home just about the time of your new child.
3. You're desperately needed at home.
4. You can, with a little effort and energy, be an engaged and loving dad.

The Test of Time

I had the privilege of working alongside Dr. James Dobson for nearly twenty years, nine as his radio cohost of the National Radio Hall of Fame broadcast, *Focus on the Family*. In the countless hours we spent in the studio together, there was one topic of conversation he loved to return to time and again: the challenge a father faces to take the long view of life as a dad and to balance his time and priorities. Allow me to share his poignant words:[2]

Let me ask you to project yourself momentarily to the end of your days, perhaps many years from now.

What will give you the greatest satisfaction as you lie there on your sickbed, thinking about the experiences of a lifetime? Will your heart thrill to the memory of honors, degrees, and professional accolades? Will fame be most highly prized, even if you manage to achieve it? Will you swell with pride over the money you've made, the books you have written, or the buildings and businesses that bear your name?

I think not.

Temporal successes and accomplishments will not be very gratifying in that moment of destiny. I believe the greatest sense of fulfillment as you prepare to close the final chapter will be in knowing that you lived by a consistent standard of holiness before God and that you invested yourself unselfishly in the lives of your family members and friends. Most important, knowing that you led your children to the Lord and will be with them in eternity will outrank every other achievement. All else will fade into insignificance. If that is a true representation of how you will feel when your days are growing short, why not determine to live according to that value system now, while you still have the opportunity to influence the impressionable kids who look up to you? This may be the most important question you as . . . father will ever be asked to answer!

Not only is spiritual development of relevance to eternity, it is also critical to the way your children will live out their days on this earth. Specifically, boys need to be well established in their faith in order to understand the meaning of good and evil. They are growing up in a postmodern world in which all ideas are considered equally valid and nothing is really wrong. Wickedness is bad only in the minds of those who think it is bad. People who live by this godless outlook on life are headed for great pain and misery. The Christian worldview, by contrast, teaches that good and evil are determined by the God of the universe and that He has given us an unchanging moral standard by which to live. He also offers forgiveness from sins, which boys (and girls) have good reason to need. Only with this understanding is a child being prepared to face the challenges that lie ahead. Yet most American children receive no spiritual training whatsoever! They are left to make it up as they go along, which leads to the meaningless existence we have discussed.

So what are you going to do about making time with your child a priority? Determine right now to do one thing every day to engage in the life of that precious child you are entrusted with. Decide to engage with your baby in meaningful ways. Make a plan, stick to it, and I can promise this: You'll be glad you did.

Suggested Resources

Overcoming Fatigue, by Paul C. Reisser, M.D. (Focus on the Family).

Margin: Restoring Emotional, Physical, Financial, and Time Reserves to Overloaded Lives, Revised, by Richard A. Swenson, M.D. (NavPress).

Sixty-Minute Family, by Rob Parsons (Lion).

Chapter 4

Break the Chain

Habit, if not resisted, soon becomes necessity.
—ST. AUGUSTINE

IN THIS CHAPTER we'll learn how to recognize and recover from your father's mistakes. Divorce and distance cause many men to learn poor patterns from their fathers. Even for guys who grow up in solid, intact homes, there will be inherited negatives. Those experiences affect our parenting approach. For those who want to leave the past behind and start fresh, this chapter provides ways to break those chains and begin new, healthy patterns.

By the time Michael Douglas married Diandra Luker in 1977, the son of screen legend Kirk Douglas was already a star in his own right. Appearing alongside Karl Malden in the hit television show *The Streets of San Francisco* thirty-three-year-old Michael appeared to have the world in the palm of his hand.

Fourteen years older than his new wife, the dashing couple gave birth to a son, Cameron, just one year later. When Cameron was just two, the new father suffered a serious skiing accident. Sidelined by the injury, his career took off again in 1984 when he starred in the hit movie *Romancing the Stone*. Douglas was already famous, but now he was rich and in demand. Studios called daily with enticing offers. He soon found himself on the road and on the set far more than at home. Although he didn't divorce his wife, Diandra, until 2000, the two basically lived separate lives, and their son, Cameron, was raised in a single-parent home. Michael struggled with alcohol and drugs and entered rehab in 1992.

A cynic might suggest this was the typical Hollywood debacle. Perhaps, but behind those sad headlines you usually find a family and a string of broken hearts. Not every child from a single-parent home abuses drugs and alcohol, but Michael's son, Cameron, did—and he found himself in and out of rehabilitation programs starting at age thirteen.

I'm sure Cameron Douglas didn't think he'd have the same problems as his dad. Cameron was raised with nearly every advantage imaginable: a great house, excellent education, exciting travel, and every toy and gadget he wanted. What he was missing was something money can't buy—a full-time father. When Cameron was on trial for illegal drug use, the elder Douglas said his family's fame and history of substance abuse helped drive his son into drug addiction and crime.

In a handwritten letter to the federal judge handling the

case, the father captured some thoughts about his son's diffi-culties that led to his drug troubles.

"I have some idea of the pressure of finding your own identity with a famous father," wrote Douglas. "I'm not sure I can comprehend it with two generations to deal with."

As the only child of a "bad marriage" between an often-absent Douglas and his wife, "Cameron found his family in the gang mentality," his father wrote.

But Judge Richard Berman discounted such reasons and pronounced a stern judgment. "Get beyond and get over that idea . . . that Cameron Douglas is a victim," Berman said.

Victim of circumstances, of his own poor choices—or is Cameron Douglas a tragic example of what happens when a father fails to model life skills and pass along values to live by?

Yearning for Dad

Many men struggle to break free of a hard life. For Cameron Douglas, a combination of an absent father, a family history of drugs and alcohol, and a series of bad choices left him with a prison sentence and plenty of time to evaluate his life. If one day he marries and has children, Cameron will have to break the chain of difficulty that has wrapped itself around his life. He will need to figure out a way to deal with his past and face the pres-ent in a healthier way—for his sake and that of his kids.

Many individuals can identify with at least some of the frac-tured Douglas heritage. We may have had hard-driving dads who expected a lot from us. Perhaps our father was not around much and did not connect emotionally with his children. We tend to approach parenting as we experienced it. As we grow up, we assemble a collection of tools, and when we have chil-dren of our own, we reach into that toolbox and use those tools with our children. That's a truth we need to consider.

Whether we grew up with a loving father or not, every parent is human. Despite good intentions, all men make mistakes that affect their kids. Every one of us takes baggage into our adult lives. These affect our parenting, so it is wise to consider what we've learned from our dad, and how that may influence our own fathering.

Learning from Dad

As sons, like it or not, we learn our approach to parenting from our parents—especially our dad. As we grow up, we mimic him in many ways. We watch him shave, and we shave like he did. We see him fixing a broken dryer, and we learn at his side about mechanical things. When we have kids of our own, we'll tend to be a lot like our dad—for the good and for the bad.

Consciously or not, you and I grab hold of our father's parenting style. It's what we use as a template for our own parenting. If there were good interactions and attitudes, we copied them and have those in our parenting toolbox. If Dad brought a thoughtful, calm, and caring approach, I'll likely emulate him. If he took time to be with me, I'll likely do the same with my kids. If he yelled a lot, my children will probably often hear me raise my voice. If he was absent or angry or distant, I'll naturally be like that with my children. You and I receive a heritage from our father that we, in turn, incorporate into our own parenting.

My Own Life

My dad has many wonderful traits. He was fun, principled, and supportive. He was an advocate for his kids and stood up for us whenever there was a problem at school or in the neighborhood.

I recall one meeting he had with a music teacher who

made disparaging comments about me—to the entire class. She really embarrassed me, and Dad took her to task.

Another time when I was about nine, Dad started a Little League alternative for boys who, like me, didn't qualify for a baseball team in the more competitive league. He watched out for me, and I've tried to emulate that value in my fathering journey.

Fortunately, I've not had to confront a teacher for unprofessional conduct, but I have had to talk with an adult for inappropriately criticizing one of my kids. That desire to protect and defend my children is inside me because I saw my own father model those values.

Nobody Is Perfect

If good parenting values can be caught and taught, it makes sense that not-so-healthy habits might also become part of our routine.

Growing up with a German-Irish father, I learned to use my voice to express anger. Raise the volume, increase the intensity, and be forceful . . . and you've got a common reaction to mistakes, irritations, and such in our home. Despite my best wishes, I found early in our marriage—and even more as a new dad—that whenever I was angry I sounded a lot like my father. Even mild irritation came out with a strong verbal barrage. It took a few years for me to recognize this pattern (despite my wife's best efforts) and to try to tone things down.

A colleague tells the story of his own father, a wonderful man but a guy with a very reserved, methodical manner. He was fun, but quiet. When my friend married a woman from a loud and spirited family, he was often ribbed for being too buttoned-down. But why shouldn't he be? To him, that was the definition of a good, responsible father. What he saw in his wife's family was zaniness. "I can't tell you how often I'm reminded to lighten up!" he says.

When it comes to inheriting parenting habits, the good will always come with the bad, and the bad will always come with the good. The secret is to find the right balance. Look back. Try to identify patterns. Take a piece of paper and write the top five good things your parents did—and then five things you didn't like. There's a good chance you'll do a little of both.

Especially if you need to break the chain, becoming self-aware is the key.

When Dad Is Divorced

Of all the negative influences affecting today's dads, divorce is probably the most pervasive and most serious. The statistics about divorce and children are sobering in several ways.

Divorce affects a startling number of children. According to a 2002 report by the US Centers for Disease Control, more than one-third of first marriages last less than ten years. And if the couple was cohabiting and not married, the chance that they'd stay together for even three years dropped to less than one in three. Second marriages were even less likely to last than first marriages. A painful number of children will see their parents' marriage break apart, and many of those will watch their dad or mom try again at marriage, only to divorce a second time.

If there's any doubt that divorce leaves deep, lasting scars, consider these sobering numbers. In a recent listing of US divorce statistics, the website for *Divorce Magazine*, which claims to "offer help for generation 'ex'," admits that:

Fatherless homes account for 63% of youth suicides, 90%

of homeless/runaway children, 85% of children with behavior problems, 71% of high school dropouts, 85% of youths in prison, well over 50% of teen mothers.[3]

Divorce affects a significant number of children, and those effects last a lifetime, following children into adulthood and coloring their parenting efforts.

When Dad Is Distant

Distance is an influence that leaves many men searching for their fathers, and affecting their own parenting.

His father was distant due to busyness and his own emotional issues, so Cameron Douglas struggled. "Cameron . . . idolized his father and did not want to be apart from him," wrote Diandra Douglas, even as she described her husband as an absent father. Michael Douglas admitted Cameron's drug use and poor life choices were because, perhaps unconsciously, he was looking for the father figure he did not have.

Children have a deep need to know their fathers, and to know a dad's love and protection. I've seen that when that connection is missing—particularly due to rejection and emotional distance—a man spends much of his life looking . . . for acceptance, for affirmation, for encouragement, for significance. These men seek what they're missing from their dad through achievement, accomplishments, and other people.

It's not hard to see why many younger people don't value marriage—it's an institution they've often seen poorly modeled. Those of us who care for the family must put more effort into helping prevent marital breakups, especially starting with younger couples. When kids grow up without a loving father, their lives are often filled with pain.

Dreaming of a Father

This distance from dad profoundly affected President Barack Obama. He wrote a book detailing his emotional quest to reach out to his father and has made one of the aims of his presidency to help repair the black traditional nuclear family. The lack of a strong father figure in the president's life is one reason he had the passion and drive to seek one of the most powerful—and most demanding—jobs around. It also explains his commitment to his wife and two daughters—a positive role model for all of us.

Often the impact isn't as positive. Author and speaker Josh McDowell[4] had an incredibly painful childhood—and a dad who was distant due to alcohol addiction. As Josh was growing up in a small town, his dad was the town drunk and everybody knew it. Josh was embarrassed and said he hated his dad so much, he wanted to kill him.

The anger festered a long time, until Josh accepted Christ as his personal Savior. "God's love took that hatred, turned it upside down, and emptied it out," Josh later wrote. "I looked my father in the eyes and said, 'Dad, I love you,' and I really meant it."

Some time passed and his dad came for a visit. "It was one of his few sober days," Josh remembers. "Dad paced nervously around the room and finally blurted out, 'Son, how can you love a father like me?'"

Josh replied, "Dad, six months ago I despised you . . . [but] I have placed my trust in Christ, received God's forgiveness, and invited Him into my life. He has changed me. God has taken away my hatred and now I love and accept you just the way you are."

His father listened and chatted warmly and finally said, "Son, if God can do in my life what I've seen Him do in yours, then I want to trust Him as my Savior and Lord."

Josh says his father's conversion stuck.

Solutions

Whether because of divorce or distance, a man who has had a difficult or nonexistent relationship with his father isn't doomed to repeat the past. Regardless of your circumstances, you can be different from your father. To break the chains and be the dad you want to be, you'll need to identify those chains and then be very intentional about getting free from them.

For many, you will need to get professional help. The wounds and difficulties run deep. Serious issues require external intervention. If that's your situation, I encourage you to immediately seek out a caring and credentialed Christian counselor who can walk you through the issues of a troubled relationship with your father.

Many books have been written about the common problems men deal with, especially those related to the patterns picked up from our dads. At the end of this chapter, I listed a few of the more helpful books and resources.

For most men, healing is possible with some honest soul-searching, thoughtful reflection, and hard work. Let me suggest the following steps as a starting point for you to learn to break the chains of poor parenting so you can become a great dad:

1. Assess your baggage.
2. Begin to address your issues.
3. Change your ways, every day.

Let's unpack these three practical points.

Assess Your Baggage

There are reasons you tend to think and act certain ways. Understanding those reasons is key to breaking the chain and becoming the dad you want to be. An assessment of the relationship you had—or didn't have—with your dad is an important step on your fathering journey. It'll involve some memories and some soul-searching.

Understanding who you are, and why, is a critical first step in being a better dad.

Ken Canfield, an expert on fathering, suggests six questions to determine what baggage you're bringing into your role as a new dad:

1. In reflecting on your relationship to your father or father figure, how would you describe his support of you?
2. Did he regularly show you affection?
3. Was he present and accessible to you growing up?
4. Did he struggle with substance abuse or was he unfaithful to your mother?
5. Did he abuse you or another family member?
6. Would you say he was a good example?[5]

These questions probe your childhood so you can recognize how your dad has influenced you. His time with you (or lack of time) and the way he treated you made an impression. Regardless of the specifics of your circumstances, you are a product of your father's parenting.

What did you feel when you read these questions? Was it uncomfortable to go back and think through the good and the bad aspects of your relationship with your dad? Maybe painful? Or perhaps you're one of the few men who have nothing but good memories of your childhood? Your answers will help you assess your fathering DNA.

Many men have serious issues that need some level of professional counseling. Maybe you can relate to the terrible strife that Josh McDowell endured, or maybe you never knew your dad at all. Perhaps you have painful wounds from your childhood that will never "just go away," and no amount of reflection and assessment seems to help. If so, I suggest you connect with a counselor at a local church, or that you find a licensed Christian counselor who can walk you through the difficulties of your past. I've listed a few resources for you at the end of this chapter.

Begin to Address Your Issues

If you've identified some of the father chains you've inherited, take the next step and address those issues.

For starters, I recommend you seek out a group of men in whom you can confide. Many churches facilitate such gatherings. It's extremely helpful to be part of a community of men who work things out together. Over the years I've participated in several groups, both formal and informal. These guys played a pivotal role in helping me become a better person and a better dad. They accepted me, listened to my questions about difficult matters, and shared in my battles.

I was the youngest man in one group, and learned a lot from the older guys who often spoke about their parenting mistakes. They did so with some regret, but also with hope that I'd get it and become a better dad by avoiding those common missteps.

A small community of like-minded men can provide a safe forum. If there is authenticity and candor, these men can form strong bonds and provide a sense of brotherhood. In addition, the biblical concept of "iron sharpening iron" can play out, allowing you to benefit from the tough but caring voice of someone who knows where you're at and who is committed to helping you become a better man.

Let me also suggest you seek out the help of an older, wiser man. A seasoned perspective can bring understanding you'd otherwise miss. I've wondered why so few of us seek out and learn from more experienced, wiser men around us. Somebody once suggested that older people have all the answers—it's just up to us to ask the right questions!

Change Your Ways, Every Day

Simply knowing about your shortcomings, without taking tangible action, won't do anything beneficial. You'll only become frustrated if you don't make something happen.

The adage is true: A journey of a thousand miles begins with one step. So start the journey to become the dad you long to be today by changing your ways—or, more specifically, changing just *one* way *this* day.

Rather than be overwhelmed by your deficiencies in the dad department, take on just one area in which you can improve—and see what you can do to make some changes.

Look through an inventory of who you are and—in light of your history—how you are likely to parent. Then list the things you don't want to do as a dad, whether that is yelling, being aloof, or escaping fathering responsibilities by loving your work too much. Map out the ways you tend to deal with life, specifically tie them to parenting, and then pick some ways to leave those chains behind.

Determine now that you'll step away for a few minutes when you sense yourself getting frustrated by your child. Or make it a point to talk every day with your wife about the baby—and how things are going for you as parents. You get the idea. The only way to break free from the shackles is to be discerning and deliberate.

Nobody is perfect, and there are no fail-safe methods when trying to break free from our past. So cut yourself—and those you love—some slack. What's important is that, when things go awry, we forgive our spouse or children, or ask to be forgiven ourselves. Pray for wisdom and discernment.

Simply acknowledging the need to break free from bad habits is the first and most important step.

Suggested Resources

Breaking the Cycle of Divorce: How Your Marriage Can Succeed Even if Your Parents' Didn't, by John Trent (Focus on the Family).

Adult Children of Divorce: Haunting Problems and Healthy Solutions, by Karen Sandvig (Thomas Nelson).

Putting Your Past Behind You: Finding Hope for Life's Deepest Hurts, by Erwin W. Lutzer (Moody Publishers).

Wisdom Chaser: Finding My Father at 14,000 Feet, by Nathan Foster (IVP Books).

Finding Home, by Jim Daly (David C. Cook).

Stronger, by Jim Daly (David. C. Cook).

The Father Connection: How You Can Make the Difference in Your Child's Self-Esteem and Sense of Purpose, by Josh McDowell (B&H Books).

To Own a Dragon: Reflections on Growing Up without A Father, by Donald Miller and John MacMurray (NavPress).

Father Fiction: Chapters for a Fatherless Generation, by Donald Miller (Howard Books).

Who's Your Daddy Now?: The Cry of a Generation in Pursuit of Fathers, by Doug Stringer (GateKeeper Publishing).

When You've Been Wronged: Moving from Bitterness to Forgiveness, by Erwin W. Lutzer (Moody Publishers).

Fatherless America, by David Blankenhorn (Harper-Perennial).

The Heart of a Father: How You Can Become a Dad of Destiny, by Ken Canfield (Northfield Publishing).

Websites:

American Association of Christian Counselors: www.aacc.net/resources/find-a-counselor

Chapter 5

How a Baby Affects Your Marriage

Babies are always more difficult than you thought—and more wonderful.
—CHARLES OSGOOD

THIS CHAPTER DISCUSSES how a baby will affect your relationship with your wife, and what to expect as she makes the transition to being a mom. Your marriage can survive a newborn!

We had been married almost four years when three simple words, "It's a boy!" changed our lives.

Overnight, our date nights were history—at least that's how I felt at the time. As new parents, we were overwhelmed, exhausted, and insecure. We kept waiting for life to return to normal, but it never did.

After two more kids, life began to spin out of control.

Our ultimate romantic fantasy was eight hours of uninterrupted sleep.

I'm not kidding.

Practical Advice

A strong desire for sleep, not romance, is what David and Claudia Arp recalled about their first baby. The Arps are counselors who have written about having a good marriage—in spite of having a baby. Their experience is universal. Most new parents feel like they've been blindsided by their baby.

David and Claudia have boiled down their advice to seven healthy habits. Take a look and see how you're doing.

1. Be deliberate in sharing responsibilities: Every family is different, but it's important to make sure one parent, usually the mother, is not the new baby's sole caretaker. If she is bearing the brunt of it, a wise man offers to shop, cook, and clean around the house.

2. Develop healthy sleep habits: Without proper rest, parents grow edgy and irritable. They don't think clearly. Try to establish a routine that will allow each parent to get some uninterrupted rest. Granted the first few weeks will be tough, but things should soon even out.

3. Find time for each other: One of my biggest mistakes was assuming I was done with dating my wife. Ironically, there is probably no better time to be deliberate about dating your spouse than after a new baby arrives. Plan ahead. Get a babysitter, even if it's for an hour's walk around the neighborhood.

4. Talk and listen effectively: This advice applies to any married couple, but it's especially important when Junior arrives. Don't assume your spouse can read your mind, and don't assume you can do the same. Ask questions—and listen to her answers!

5. Make your love life a priority: Romance didn't rank high on my list those first weeks with a new baby—and you can be sure my wife was interested even less. But it's important to carve out time. Be creative and spontaneous. Perhaps a friend can watch the baby at their house—and instead of going out, the two of you can stay in.

6. Grow together spiritually: It's easy to let Scripture study and prayer time together slide when you're exhausted and trying to find your way as a new father. But as with dating, this is a time when you need the Lord's wisdom most. Even if you read only a passage or two, keep reading your Bible. Pray simple prayers together. Pray for each other—and pray for this wonderful new life!

7. Nurture your relationship: Do you remember why you fell in love with your spouse? Maybe it's time to write her a letter and remind her. (Perhaps you'll benefit from the recollection too.) Don't forget that it's often the little things, like bringing her coffee in bed or bringing home flowers for no reason, that make the biggest impression.

Chris and Jessica's Story

Consider Chris and Jessica. Chris is a successful video producer who has abundant energy, and Jessica is a graphic designer. They're a fun couple to be around. They married in their mid-thirties and soon had a child. Now two and a half, that little bundle named Ethan affected their marriage in several ways.

There was certainly a physical impact. Jessica is petite, and carrying her preborn child was a significant strain on her tiny body. After Ethan's arrival, her postpartum weight loss came easily, although Jessica's energy levels took longer to recover. In fact, these days she's pretty tired. Lately Ethan tends to get up a couple of times per night, and that's cut into Chris and Jessica's sleep. They're big coffee lovers now, depending on the caffeine to keep them going throughout the day. They don't remember the last time they had a good night's sleep.

Chris and Jessica's sexual relationship has been altered by their general lack of physical stamina, this interrupted sleep schedule, and Ethan's other ongoing needs. These days, going to bed at 8 p.m. seems like a good idea—and that's so they can sleep . . . nothing more.

The kind of romance they enjoyed regularly has been relegated to special occasions. Despite their desires to resume that part of their life, it's just not happening. This is just a season, they tell themselves, and they both look forward to when they'll be getting more sleep and have the sexual intimacy they once enjoyed.

Emotionally, Jessica and Chris will tell you they're doing okay. They're settling into their parental roles, adjusting to the demands of parenting. Chris gets encouragement in his fathering from the guys at work, and several of them are in a similar season. He still has time to play football on weekends.

Jessica is developing a new graphics business out of their home, and is often caught up in the busyness of that. Still, she makes time for her friends and gets a gals' night out every few weeks. So they feel like they're getting some quality time to keep sane.

Truthfully, though, some struggles are going on below the surface. Jessica is consumed by Ethan's needs, and seems unavailable for Chris when he comes home in the evenings. They used to have some great talk time, but now that's gone. Jessica is usually less interested in what happened in Chris's day, and much more interested in what Ethan did, or how he is feeling. And Chris is starting to resent that.

Practically, while Ethan needs diapers and baby food, there hasn't yet been a huge financial hit. Around the house, certainly they've had to baby-proof the place, but it's been a pretty natural adjustment for them. Besides, it is kind of fun to have this bundle of joy and energy . . . these days he's always exploring and is learning so much!

One area of life they're having a bit of trouble with is "together time." While they pursue their separate interests and hobbies, Chris and Jessica aren't doing as much together as they used to. It's hard, because Ethan is at a particularly demanding stage. As a toddler, he tends to get into things around the house, makes messes, and needs a lot of supervision. His bedtime is so early, Chris and Jessica can't get out for dates—and besides, who can they trust to take care of the baby? They're concerned with his safety and well-being, so finding a trustworthy babysitter seems impossible.

Does this sound familiar? It will.

Chris and Jessica's story may be yours.

They're the poster couple for a simple truth: *Your marital relationship will change significantly when your baby comes.*

Changing Roles

For many couples, getting married is fun, exciting, and relatively easy compared to the shift to being parents. The changes from dating to engaged took several months and didn't require too much energy. Then came the steps to becoming husband and wife, another rather natural progression. The journey together led to wonderful conversations and a shared sense of oneness. So it is a surprise when couples find themselves angry, tired, and retreating into their own worlds when Junior is born.

At the risk of stating the obvious, maintaining that marital bond while adjusting to caring for a baby is usually fairly difficult. Numerous issues arise, from emotional to physical. The key to doing well as a husband and as a dad is expecting things to be hard—and dealing well with the conflicts and challenges.

What to Expect

Be prepared for a shift in thinking. When you take on that parental title and its attendant responsibilities, a mental change takes place. Once you were husband and wife; now you're husband-and-wife *and* dad-and-mom. You used to fully devote your relational attention to each other; now you have a third party in the family who will demand a lot.

The shift to being a mom and dad is huge, and it requires some serious juggling. What was once a "100 percent you and me" perspective is now less clean and simple. Is it a "50 percent for you and 50 percent for the baby" relationship? Maybe. It's dangerous and arbitrary to try to quantify relationships by percentages. For some, a 50 percent statistic would be welcome. I guess most men feel they have 20 percent access to their wife's time and energy.

Most women have a superstrong nurturing instinct that kicks in when baby arrives, and it becomes foremost in their minds. The urge to invest fully in that child is overwhelming! It doesn't mean she wants to neglect you, her dear husband, it's just that the baby needs her.

The more you understand this, the easier it will be for you to manage the changes.

One excellent way to better prepare for or deal with the reality of divided loyalties is to work on your communication. Make sure you and your wife talk often. Plan on that weekly date night, so the two of you can have some good, uninterrupted conversation. And talk about more than just the baby! Try to reserve those talks for another time. Your date time should be all about the two of you, with some fun and some memory-making.

But What about the Baby?
(We can't leave the baby with someone yet.)

Sharing babysitting duties with friends who also have a newborn is a great and economical way to manage these early days of parenting. This is something we learned when we had our fourth, and I wished we had done this much sooner.

We eventually got into a great routine of having regular talk times. Every Friday was date night—one week for us, the next for the other couple. When it was our turn to get away, Joan would come to our place so the kids could have their regular foods and beds. We'd go out for the evening confident that an experienced, caring mom we really trusted was in control of our children. No worries! The next week Dena would go to their place (while I managed our kids at our house), and James and Joan would head off for dinner or a hike.

When you trade babysitting responsibilities with like-minded friends, you receive something even more valuable than safe and affordable child care. You'll enjoy the company and perspective of other parents who are going through the same season of life. You've heard "there's safety in numbers"? There's comfort too.

Life Is Changing—for the Better

Most of our discussion in this chapter has dealt with the practical side of managing the arrival of a new child. Having experienced this six times, I can confidently declare this:

If handled deliberately and carefully, the arrival of a child into your marriage will indeed forever change your union—but only for the better. Looking back on life without children, I can honestly say our lives have improved by nearly every measure.

Life is more fun, and it has more meaning. Having been forced to reckon with my selfish proclivities, I've grown as a man. My walk with the Lord has become more steady. In my wife's mothering, I see God's goodness. And in our children, I see His wonder and majesty.

Yes, a baby will affect your marriage, because a baby will change you in miraculous and mighty ways.

5 Tips

to Help Your Marriage
Survive a New Baby

1. Stay connected with your wife. Make room in your schedule for daily talk times and weekly dates. Do things together as a family. Hang out at the park with parents who also have young kids. Develop routines like Thursday night pizza or Sunday afternoons. Take family hikes or bike rides.

2. Remember that your wife is not your enemy. She is the love of your life, and you need to treat her as your shining jewel. So don't get angry with her. Don't blow up when she is exhausted and really needs you to help out. Extend lots of grace. Follow the scriptural admonition to be "quick to listen, slow to speak and slow to become angry" (James 1:19).

3. Remember that this child is not your enemy. You love this little baby, really you do! So don't for a minute think she is an enemy to your marriage. Yes, she will demand a lot of you, and she will extract a lot of your wife's energies and attentions. But she's your child, and you have a tremendous responsibility to raise her well. It's your job to allow her needs to dictate a lot of your and your wife's choices and activities—for now. And that will impact your marriage.

4. Share the load. Now is the time to show your wife you love her by sacrificing your pride—or your stubbornness—and really stepping up the contribution you make to her life. Clean the kitchen or her car. Empty the trash. Change that baby's diaper. Make dinner. Those domestic duties need to be shared, as she is pretty tired from being a mom. Come alongside her and help. Look around, find practical things that need to be done, and get to work. Your wife will notice, even if she doesn't say anything right now.

5. Get some sleep. Take turns wearing earplugs. Seriously. Buy some Mack's Silicone Earplugs and learn to love 'em! I didn't want to consider earplugs, but Dena started using them and it became apparent she was sleeping well—while I didn't, because our son kept waking me during the night. When you are desperate for sleep, wear earplugs. Alternate turns, so at least one of you gets a good night of rest, every night.

Suggested Resources

Your Marriage Can Survive a Newborn, by Glenn and Natalie Williams (B&H).

Becoming Parents: How to Strengthen Your Marriage as Your Family Grows, by Pamela Jordan, Scott Stanley, Howard Markman (John Wiley & Sons).

Now What? The Chapman Guide to Marriage after the Children Arrive, by Gary Chapman (Tyndale House).

Chapter 6

Loving
Your Wife

Let the wife make the husband glad to come home,
and let him make her sorry to see him leave.
—MARTIN LUTHER

YOUR WIFE'S TIME and energy are about to
be radically adjusted. Are you ready for the
emotional and physical changes coming your
way? This chapter offers suggestions for
navigating the sometimes confusing days
ahead, including what to expect in your
sexual relationship.

Several years ago, the editors of the *Abilene Reporter-News*, a daily paper in Texas, asked its readers to submit the best advice they had received from their fathers. The vignettes were published on Father's Day.

The newsroom was flooded with responses and could publish only a small portion of what they received. Most respondents shared very practical advice. One was grateful his father warned him about the evils of smoking and chewing tobacco. Another spoke of his father's example of "honest pay for honest and hard work." Yet another wrote simply and bluntly, "Dynamite comes in small packages!"

Debbie Stanford of Coleman, Texas, offered a more reflective and deeper contribution:

> Daddy, Buster Donham, wrote in my son's Bible on his first Father's Day: "What it means to be a father to me: It was a good life to watch my girls grow up. There were lots of good times and some bad that I don't think about a lot. I want to tell you what I think is first. The first thing is to put God first in your life and read your Bible every day and always pray for His way in your life. Second is your family; always have time for them and love all of them. Third is your job. It takes money to keep things going and that is hard to do sometimes. The best thing I can give you kids is [to] love their mother (and your wife when you marry). Let her know every day that she comes first in your life. It takes a lot of staying on your knees and a lot of whispered prayers and love to raise kids. Because they walk in your footsteps and live what they see.

I never had the pleasure of meeting Buster, but I'm confident we'll cross paths on the other side. He's uncovered one of the great secrets to a good life. You've heard the expression, "Happy wife, happy life"? Although it's often spoken in jest, many a truth is packed in humorous asides. We'll deal with some common misperceptions about love and happiness.

The Slippery Slope

Have you ever made a New Year's resolution, only to break it by the first week of January? Somebody once said the road to hell is paved with good intentions. The same might be so for tackling your new role as a father. I'm reminded of a *Saturday Evening Post* article titled, "The Seven Ages of the Married Cold." The essayists chronicled the typical progression of a husband's reaction to his wife's sickness. See if this sounds familiar:

The first year: "Sugar dumpling, I'm really worried about my baby girl. You've got a bad sniffle, and there's no telling about these things with all this strep throat going around. I'm putting you in the hospital this afternoon for a general checkup and a good rest. I know the food's lousy, but I'll be bringing your meals in from Rosini's. I've already got it all arranged with the floor superintendent."

The second year: "Listen, darling, I don't like the sound of that cough. I called Doc Miller and asked him to rush over here. Now you go to bed like a good girl, please? Just for Papa."

The third year: "Maybe you'd better lie down, honey: nothing like a little rest when you feel lousy. I'll bring you something to eat. Have you got any canned soup?"

The fourth year: "Now look, dear, be sensible. After you've fed the kids, washed the dishes, and finished the floor, you'd better lie down."

The fifth year: "Why don't you take a couple of aspirin?"

The sixth year: "I wish you'd just gargle or something, instead of sitting around all evening barking like a seal!"

The seventh year: "For Pete's sake, stop sneezing! Are you trying to give me pneumonia?"

While there is a degree of comedy in this exchange, the underlying theme points to a real problem. As husbands, we would be wise to print or type out the apostle Paul's famous words to the church at Ephesus:

> Husbands, love your wives, just as Christ loved the church and gave himself up for her to make her holy, cleansing her by the washing with water through the word, and to present her to himself as a radiant church, without stain or wrinkle or any other blemish, but holy and blameless. (Ephesians 5:25–27)

What Does It *Really* Mean to Love?

It's not a trick question, but the answer is probably more complicated than conventional wisdom would suggest. If you were to ask ten husbands what it means to love their wives, nine out of ten would offer some version of "make them happy." Although extending kindness to our wives is an essential component of marriage, our faith suggests something more.

In his powerful book *The Problem of Pain*, C. S. Lewis tackles this matter head-on. He wrote, "By Love . . . most of us mean kindness—the desire to see others than the self happy; not happy in this way or in that, but just happy."[6]

Okay, I know I'm guilty of embracing that philosophy! But Lewis concludes, "God does not govern the universe on such lines. And since God is Love, I conclude that my conception of love needs correction."

I suddenly don't feel so bad. If someone like C. S. Lewis admits needing a theological tune-up on love, perhaps I shouldn't be so surprised that I also need one. Alas, if love is not about making our spouse happy, what is it all about? Lewis provides perspective on Paul's writings:

> Love demands the perfecting of the beloved; that the mere "kindness" which tolerates anything except suffering in its object is, in that respect, at the opposite pole from Love.

In other words, my job as a husband in loving my wife is to simply try to help her become the woman God intended.

How?

How can we, as husbands (as the US Army used to ask of their recruits), help our wives become "all that they can be"? Scripture provides advice. In the first book of Peter, we're told to "be considerate as you live with your wives " (1 Peter 3:7). We're called to know them, their likes and dislikes, their pet peeves, and the things they love and love doing.

The other day when I came home from work, I greeted my wife, and after our kiss and the usual "How was your day?" I asked, "Do you have a headache?"

"Yes," she answered, with a smirk.

How did I know? I've lived with Dena for twenty-six years, and I've learned to read her facial expressions. And her face told me her head was hurting. It's a simple example, but we men would do well to apply some of our brain power to knowing and understanding our spouse. She'll appreciate it, and when we perform that simple act of observing, remembering, and caring, we'll show her love.

You might be thinking, *Okay, I get it. God's not calling me to help keep my wife entertained and happy, like I'm some sort of clown at a kid's birthday party. But what can I do to help accomplish my goal of really loving my wife?* Let's end with a dose of practicality, a few suggestions drawn from a variety of people and sources. As I tell people when they ask about me recommending the perfect running shoe, there is no perfect suggestion—only the suggestion that's perfect for you.

1. Start or end each day by holding hands and praying together with your wife.
2. Talk to her respectfully without demeaning her or hurting her feelings.
3. Show interest in her friends—and give her time to be with them.
4. Express to her that you need and value her.
5. Show enthusiasm for the things that she's excited about—let your actions show it.
6. Find something that makes you laugh together.
7. Put your arms around her when she needs comfort, holding her silently.
8. Surprise her by doing, before she asks, something you think she would want done.
9. Try not to make sudden changes without discussing them with her first.
10. Show interest in that which she values.
11. Allow your wife to teach you things without becoming defensive.
12. Let go of the small stuff. We all have annoying habits and preferences that differ from our spouse's.
13. Go shopping with her and don't sigh or check the time even once.

14. Make the time with her to set specific goals to achieve together for each year.
15. Be polite, courteous, and mannerly with her—not taking her for granted.
16. Exhibit humility, admit your mistakes, and ask for forgiveness. She'll appreciate that!
17. Don't belittle her intelligence.
18. Scratch her back, rub her feet, or her rub her neck—whatever she prefers.
19. Get up in the middle of the night (letting her stay in bed) to take care of your upset child.
20. Be especially helpful when she doesn't feel well.
21. When you've been apart for a time and she asks how your day went, don't just say "fine"; give her details.
22. Thank God for her by name when the two of you pray together.
23. Try not to argue over money. Instead, peacefully discuss future expenditures.
24. Don't embarrass her by arguing with her in front of others.
25. Lead your family in their spiritual relationship with God. This is important to her.
26. Stay away from websites, online content, or anything that gives you sexual gratification from anyone other than your wife.
27. Be helpful and cooperative before and during the time you have other people over to your home. (If you're not sure what to do, ask your wife, "What can I do that would help the most?")
28. Brag about her to others—both in front of her and when she is not with you.
29. Surprise her from time to time with a card and flowers or a little gift.

30. Tell her or call her as soon as you know you are going to be late.
31. Give her your undivided attention when she wants to talk.
32. Maintain good grooming habits so you look and smell good. It shows you care.
33. Help her to finish her education and accomplish goals that are important to her.
34. View and treat her as if God put a sign over her that says, "Make me feel special."
35. Run errands without complaining.
36. Give her the love gift of being thoughtful and considerate to her relatives.
37. Show her you are her marital partner by not making plans without her (unless it's a surprise for her).
38. Keep her trust at all costs. Leave no gray area when it comes to other female relationships, money, and your word.
39. Surprise her by asking her to give you a list of three things she'd like done around the house in the next month. Make it your goal to do them.
40. Ask her—and then listen without judging—what makes her fearful and insecure.
41. Find out her sexual needs—and then try to fulfill them.
42. Surprise her with a fifteen-second kiss (with no expectations to go any further).
43. Keep yourself in as good a shape as reasonable so she's proud to be with you.
44. Write a mission statement together for your marriage and family.
45. Show affection for her in front of friends.
46. Make a point to honor anniversaries, birthdays, and other special occasions.

47. Don't tease and belittle her, saying, "I was just joking" when she doesn't find it funny.
48. Hold her hand in public as you did when you dated her.
49. Call, email, or text her during the day when you are apart so she knows you are thinking of her.
50. Surprise her by suggesting you go to a marriage seminar or weekend retreat together to draw even closer in your marriage.

Suggested Resources

For Married Men Only: Three Principles for Loving Your Wife, by Tony Evans (Moody Publishers).

The Marriage Turnaround: How Thinking Differently about Your Relationship Can Change Everything, by Mitch Temple (Moody Publishers).

For Married Men Only, by Shaunt Feldhahn, Jeff Feldhahn (Multnomah Publishers).

Love & Respect: The Love She Most Desires, The Respect He Desperately Needs, by Dr. EmersonEggerich (Thomas Nelson).

Chapter 7

Loving Your Baby's Mother

The greatest thing you can do for
your children is to love their mother.
—THEODORE HESBURGH, PRESIDENT EMERITUS,
UNIVERSITY OF NOTRE DAME

KIDS NEED TO SEE a loving, stable marriage
as they grow up—and they'll benefit from
that modeling for years to come. This chapter
will help you support and love your wife in
ways that matter.

The ballroom in the InterContinental Hotel in Dallas was filled. At the kick-off event of Focus on the Family's Celebrate Family, Celebrate Life tour, the audience was fairly conservative and obviously committed to the well-being of their families. As part of the festivities, we were to record a *Focus on the Family* radio broadcast. Our conversation that night included Focus's president, Jim Daly; Focus family psychologist Dr. Juli Slattery; the beloved Dr. Gary Smalley; and author, speaker, and pastor Dr. Ted Cunningham.

Ted Cunningham is a friend and a man with impeccable credentials. A gifted communicator, he knows how to grab an audience. Theologically and socially, he's orthodox. But that night he said something that made the audience gasp. He wasn't dramatic about it, and at the moment I didn't think much about his comment. But there it was—and people had some strong reactions.

He told a story about his five-year-old daughter who asked him a difficult question.

"Daddy," she said, "who do you love more? Mommy or me?"

As innocent as it seems, many parents have been paralyzed by that kind of question. To a man it seems like a no-win proposition. There's no apparent right answer, and if you reply the wrong way, you could have a tough time explaining what you said. Dismiss the query and you might crush your little girl's heart.

So how do you answer a question like that?

Ted's response seemed reasonable to me. But there were audible reactions from many in the auditorium, mostly women.

"Well . . . you've got to know, sweetheart, that while I love you a whole lot, I love your mommy even more."

Suddenly a rush of thoughts came flying into the minds of

hundreds in the audience. I could almost hear them. *Wait a minute, Ted. Are you telling me you love your wife more than your child? C'mon, man, that's not what your girl wanted to hear! You've crushed her heart.* Or perhaps, *Yikes, you mean I can love my wife more than our kids?*

How did you react when you read Ted's candid answer to his little girl? Did his response startle you?

Establishing Priorities

Every family has relational priorities. For many couples, the children become the central point—it's all about the kids. It seems this is the approach to family life most valued in our culture. But while it is commonly accepted to make the kids the focus of all our efforts, I think it is wrong and shortsighted. I suggest the healthiest thing for your family is to take Ted's advice:

Love your wife more than your kids.

Who Do You Love Most?

A popular parenting website recently posed a question to readers. If any of the women responding were in that Dallas audience, they were probably the ones who gasped at Ted's answer.

The online forum asked this: "Kids or Spouse: Who do you love more?"

The answers—from women—are revealing:

I don't know. To me this question is a bit silly. I love them both equally. Does this mean my love for my two girls is the same as my love for my husband? Of course not. In fact, my love for my eldest daughter isn't the same as my love for my youngest. Each is different and special in its own way—that special bond that I only share with *that* other person.

To actually love one more than the other is silly. What is your child if not half of the person you married?

I love my kids and my spouse equally. That being said, my love for them is different. My children definitely have my unconditional love and my husband has my deep, intimate love. But my daughter could say it best: "Who do you love more, your mom or your dad? That's silly! I love them both!"

I agree with the other ladies, you can't answer this question. I love my husband in a way that I will never love another person, the type of love that is only felt between a husband and wife. I love my son in a way that all mothers love their sons, unconditionally and forever.

Many women, consciously or not, give their love fully to their children . . . leaving their husband feeling on the periphery. Call it the nurturing instinct, the mama bear syndrome, or whatever . . . most women with babies can't help but pour their entire being into that child. You're not the only guy feeling a bit odd about this.

Odd Man Out?

As a husband and dad, you can expect this kind of response from your wife. It's natural. It doesn't mean she's no longer in love with you. It doesn't mean you've messed up. It doesn't mean you'll forever be battling this little bundle of joy for your wife's heart.

Your baby is perfectly helpless and needs everything done for him, and your wife knows she is that child's primary need-meeter. Of course, you're part of that equation, but in most families it will be the mother who spends the majority of time with their infant.

While you will be helping with the baby, you'll find yourself feeling a bit like the odd man out. So you'll want to implement some new approaches to loving your wife. For the sake of your marriage and your child, you'll need to cultivate your marriage relationship.

It's natural for us as parents to pledge our all to this new little one. She is so helpless, so dependent. You want the best for your child, providing the important things for her. You want her to be safe, to know she is loved, to have the things and opportunities that can make for a happy child. You want to see her understand and embrace your values. You'll want to find her the right school. You look forward to helping her learn to read, ride a bike, catch a ball, and learn to enjoy a sunset. You'll sacrifice a lot to make life special for her. This is all fine.

I can't emphasize this enough. The one other thing you'll want to do, to help your child succeed in life, is to *really and truly love her mom*.

Research Confirms It

Over the years, research has confirmed a direct correlation between children's emotional well-being and their parents' relationship. When Dad loves Mom, kids are more secure and are healthier emotionally. In study after study, children are found to do best when raised in an intact, two-parent home. This doesn't mean that children in single-parent families are destined for disaster. But it does mean children are more likely to thrive when they don't have to try to navigate parental dysfunction.

The research reveals something else of interest. In a study

that examined millionaires in America, the social scientists
found the "typical millionaire" has these traits in common: They
worked between eight and ten hours per day for thirty years—
and remained married to the same person. In a similar study, a
New York executive search firm found that of 1,365 corporate
vice presidents, 87 percent were still married to their first wife—
and 92 percent were raised in two-parent families.

The Art of Commitment

The parenting journey demands total commitment. You've
got to be determined to do the right thing, for your child, at
the right time, for the right reasons. But that doesn't mean
you give your child 100 percent of your time, energy, and love.
If Mom is in the picture, and your marriage is to survive, you've
got to make her your priority.

What your son or daughter needs, besides your unconditional love, is the safety and security offered by your loving,
stable marriage.

Firsthand Knowledge

Even before we had our first child, I saw this dynamic at
work in our relationship. Early in our marriage my wife stayed
at home and, while her sister finished college, Dena cared for
our niece several times a week. We loved having that precious
little girl visit our home, and it was a joy to love her.

But after several weeks I began to notice that Dena would
make Mariah a priority, attending to her needs at the expense
of our time together. I watched my wife become motherly
toward our niece, pouring emotional energy into her. She lov-
ingly nurtured the child. They read books, walked to the park,
and even napped together. We structured our lives around a
two-year-old's schedule and needs. And in some ways, Dena

had a little less time and energy for me.

I had to adjust to that change. Where once I was the sole recipient of my wife's affections, I had to share her heart with Mariah. It wasn't that I was being neglected, but someone else in our home had more pressing needs. I had to willingly step aside and allow Dena to become our niece's caregiver.

Guard Your Marriage

During this season of adjustment, you'll need to step up your efforts to engage with your wife—for a number of reasons. One of the most important is to avoid temptation. If you don't handle these early days of being a parent well, especially with your wife's energies directed at the baby, you might seek out inappropriate—and ultimately damaging—attention from another woman.

That's a difficult headline we've seen time and again. We've read of too many prominent people—politicians, celebrities, sports figures—who have been more concerned with an often short-lived quest for personal "fulfillment" than for keeping their commitments to their family. Few of us will ever live in the spotlight. But even those who are not high profile need to avoid a mistake that will cause irreparable damage to your marriage—and your relationship with your child.

Long-term Perspective: Two of Us

Here's some perspective on why you'll want to love your wife even more than your kids. It won't always be "us," as in "the three (or four) of us." It will take twenty years or more, but eventually this baby will grow up. Hard to believe, but one day you'll find yourself looking into his eyes and wondering who this kid is—he's got facial hair, he isn't interested in listening to you, he thinks he's a man now. Despite a good relationship, you might actually contemplate kicking him out of the house.

When he does eventually move out, you'll still have your wife at your side. She will be your companion into your golden years. She will be the one with whom you share your daily joys in the coming seasons of life. While you'll likely stay in touch with your children, your life will revert to the "you and me." You'll reap great dividends *then* if you make sure *now* that you invest time and energy in your marriage.

As we've said good-bye to our two oldest boys, we've come to realize the value of long-term perspective. They've finished high school and are establishing their adult identities. While we're no longer their primary influencers, we're still in touch and are glad to see them when we can. But they've moved out and on—and no longer depend on us. We've learned to let go and have seen that the parenting process is ultimately about helping our kids learn to make it in life without us. And when they are gone, we have each other as primary companions, partners, and soul mates.

While we still have four children at home, the process of watching our two oldest leave helps me see the importance of keeping our marriage strong. My wife is the one person who will be the constant in my life. My kids may live nearby—or on another continent. My time with them will be limited. When our other four kids leave home, my relationship with Dena will mean everything to me.

Suggested Resources

Do Your Kids a Favor . . . Love Your Spouse, by Kendra Smiley with John Smiley (Moody Publishers).
Great Parents, Lousy Lovers: Why Your Kids Deserve to

Experience Your Great Marriage, by Gary Smalley, Ted Cunningham (Tyndale House).

Chapter 8

Boys-n-Girls

Boys will be boys. And even that wouldn't matter
if only we could prevent girls from being girls.
—ANNE FRANK

FIRST-TIME FATHERS need to know that there
are key differences between the genders. This
chapter will tell you what you need to know
about gender differences and how you can be
the dad your son or daughter needs.

Wwhen Dakota, our oldest, was two, he began having difficulty navigating certain situations. One day when we picked him up from the church nursery, the woman in charge reported, "Dakota is really causing problems here. This morning he hit a child and also bit someone. If he doesn't behave properly," she said, "he won't be able to keep coming to this nursery."

My wife cried.

It hurt to think she had failed as a parent. She was alarmed by the woman's ultimatum. She wondered how we had raised such a child. How could our son be so ill-tempered and aggressive? We tried to teach him to be kind. We didn't expose him to violent television shows.

What was wrong?

Dena discussed the "nursery incident" with another young mom at church. Dee and her husband, Scott, had three kids, all boys. She laughed about the matter.

"Oh Dena, you don't need to worry too much. Marcy only has one little girl, and she has no idea what boys are like. She thinks every child is just like her little princess—all quiet and content. Relax! Boys behave like this all the time."

In Touch with Reality!

You can imagine how comforting those words were. Unbound by unrealistic expectations about how a little boy should behave, Dena found joy in some of the distinctives that make boys . . . boys. She was unconstrained by Marcy's view that boys should be like girls.

Boys and girls *are* different. That might seem obvious, but let's consider some of the facts. As a first-time father, you'll benefit from knowing what to expect.

First, a caveat: The findings I'm about to share deal in averages. For example, conventional wisdom suggests that California is warmer than Montana. But there have been summer days when the opposite is true. The same can said about the differences between boys and girls. Boys are generally considered more aggressive, but everybody has come across a tough-as-nails girl. She is neither weird nor a freak of nature.

With that in mind, here are some general traits that you, as a first-time father, should find interesting and helpful.

Girls

Matt is a man's man. A former scholarship athlete in several collegiate sports, he's now a cabinetmaker here in Colorado Springs. A couple of years into their marriage he and his wife, Jennifer, were blessed with two boys in two years. Matt took to them like a fish to water. Wrestling matches and ball playing framed the beginning and end of each day. The three of them clicked. He felt like a good father and connected quickly with his sons. As they matured, they would regularly tease and joke with one another. All was right with the world.

Enter Jillian. The daughter his wife always wanted arrived with great fanfare. Pink and lace began popping up everywhere. Matt took her birth in stride. Not only was he happy to have a daughter but he was also thrilled that Jennifer would have a girl to help balance the household's hormonal scale. He wasn't nearly as anxious about parenting her as he was back when the boys arrived. After all, seven years ago he was a rookie—now he was an experienced veteran.

The young family of five settled into a new routine. According to Matt, he was rarely surprised in the first two years of Jillian's life. But soon after her second birthday he began to notice things were different than at that same stage with his two boys. She didn't appreciate roughhousing to the same degree and seemed quicker to tear up and slower to calm down.

The older she grew the more it struck him: parenting a daughter is going to be very different from parenting a son. After a particularly tough day of tantrums and tears he confided to a friend, "I am thoroughly confused. How she can go from laughter to crying so quickly? She is a mystery to me!"

I can relate to Matt's dilemma. When our oldest girl Allie arrived, I experienced a similar period of transition. I never expected her to be just like Dakota or Seth, and knew boys and girls were different, but I have to admit, I was a bit surprised how distinct the differences were.

Additional Distinctions

- Girls have fewer attention-span problems and can make faster transitions between lessons.
- Stronger neural connectors create better listening skills, more detailed memory storage, and better discrimination among tones of voice.
- A girl's stronger neural connectors and a larger hippocampus provide greater use of sensory memory details in speaking and writing.
- Girls' prefrontal cortex develops earlier and is larger than boys'.
- Girls have more serotonin and make fewer impulsive decisions than boys. Teenagers don't think of the consequences of their actions. They act on impulse. Serotonin and oxytocin tell a teenager to slow down and think about what could happen if they did something. Our job as adults is to serve as external frontal lobes.
- A girl's brain also experiences approximately 15 percent more blood flow.
- With more cortical areas devoted to verbal functioning, girls are better at sensory memory, sitting still, listening,

tonality, mental cross talk, and the complexities of reading and writing—the very skills and behaviors often rewarded in schools.[7]

Boys

Nicole never had a brother and in fact, spent very little time with young boys. Whenever she saw her cousins at family reunions they were on their best behavior. Her father was quiet and besides, he worked a lot of hours outside the home. She and her only sister did all the things little girls do—they played house and dress-up and hosted tea parties with their mother in the backyard. They would sit for hours and quietly read. In other words, she wasn't too familiar with the energetic nature of boys and subconsciously assumed that life with kids would look a lot like she remembered her childhood.

Nicole married, and when little Sammie was born, she cried tears of joy. A son! How wonderful! As time progressed, though, she would shed tears of frustration. It wasn't that he was ill or troubled. She was simply shocked by just how physical he was, even at a very young age. She would sit with him in his room and build large towers with bright-colored blocks. Even before the last block was in place, little Sammie would lunge forward and topple the masterpiece, laughing and giggling all the way. Forget Bob the Builder—her son was Sam the Destroyer!

As my wife, Dena, had discovered with our oldest son, Dakota, little boys like to make big messes and are often energized by dismantling pretty things. There's a very good chance that your wife "gets this" on an intellectual level—but how does it look on a day-to-day basis? Here is a brief summary of what you and she can expect:

- Boys have more cortical area devoted to spatial-mechanical functioning and half as many to verbal-emotive functioning.
- Spatial-mechanical functioning makes boys want to move objects through the air, such as balls, airplanes, their little sisters, or just their arms and legs.
- "Boys are significantly more likely to do something dangerous," writes Leonard Sax in his book *Why Gender Matters*. "Risky and dangerous activities trigger a 'fight or flight' response that gives a tingle, a charge, an excitement that many boys find irresistible. Boys systematically *overestimate* their own ability, while girls are more likely to *underestimate* their abilities."[8]
- Boys have less serotonin and less oxytocin, which makes them more impulsive and less likely to sit still to talk to someone.
- Boys have less blood flow to the brain and tend to structure or compartmentalize learning.
- The male brain is designed to go into *rest states* in which it renews, recharges, and reorients itself. (Girls can do this without going to sleep.)
- The more words a teacher uses, the more likely a boy will quit listening.
- Boys' brains are better suited to symbols, abstractions, and pictures. So boys generally learn higher math and physics better than girls. Boys prefer video games for the physical movement and destruction. And boys get into more trouble for not listening, moving around, sleeping in class, and incomplete assignments.[9]

There have now been several decades of rhetoric suggesting the only difference between the sexes is the ability to bear children. Do you think conventional wisdom might bear some revision?

Since men tend to thrive with lists and charts, on the following page there is an easy-to-use reference guide that details some of the strong neurological differences between boys and girls.

Keeping Up and Keeping On

Let me share some of the challenges Dena and I faced in keeping up with one of our boys. (I'll not identify which of our three sons was the guilty party.) One August day this three-year-old boy:

- Climbed six feet to the top shelf of his closet to grab a book.
- Turned on the video player to watch movies—without approval. Twice.
- Hacked into the kids' account on the computer so he could play a favorite game.
- Interfered with dinner by pouring a big glass of water into a pot of rice.
- Dumped out the dog's water.
- Stood by Mom as she tried to light the grill . . . and blew out the match. Twice!
- Wandered down the block until a neighbor intervened.
- Climbed into the kitchen cupboards and grabbed marshmallows and cookies . . . hiding the unauthorized snacks in his room. With a glass of milk.

Quite the list, don't you agree? And that was really a fairly routine week for this boy. All in a parent's day's work!

BRAIN-BASED GENETIC DIFFERENCES IN GIRLS AND BOYS

Girls Tend To	Boys Tend To
Have better hearing than boys and may find loud or repetitive noises distracting.	Have worse hearing than girls and may lose attention simply because they can't hear.
Be better at object discrimination. ("What is it?")	Be better at object location. ("Where is it?")
Focus on faces and things.	Focus on movement.
Use more of the "advanced" part of their brains, such as the cerebral cortex.	Use more of the "primitive" parts of their brains, the hippocampus and amygdala.
Be able to explain and describe their feelings.	Find it difficult to talk about feelings.
Be more verbal and emotive.	Be more spatial and mechanical.
Develop language and fine motor skills about six years earlier than boys.	Develop targeting and spatial memory about four years earlier than girls.
Multitask well and make easy transitions.	Focus on a task and transition more slowly.
Focus their friendships on other girls.	Focus their friendships on a shared activity.
See conversation as central to a friendship.	See conversation as often unnecessary.
Let social hierarchies destroy a friendship.	Let social hierarchies build camaraderie and organize relationships.
See self-revelation and sharing as precious parts of a friendship.	See self-revelation as something to be avoided if possible.
Often ask a teacher for help and enjoy a close relationship with a teacher.	May not ask for help to avoid being perceived as "sucking up" to a teacher.
Like to be faced, looked in the eye, and smiled at.	Avoid eye contact and prefer you sit beside them.
Retain sensory memory details well and make good distinctions between colors.	Not retain sensory details or make color distinctions as well.
Deal with moderate stress, such as timed tests, less successfully.	Deal with moderate stress well and may actually do better because of it.
Want to be with friends when under stress.	Want to be alone when under stress.
Feel "yucky" when faced with threat and confrontation.	Feel excited when faced with threat and confrontation.
Rarely employ aggression playfully.	Often employ aggression playfully.
Connect sex to other outcomes.	Focus on the sexual activity itself.
Use landmarks to give directions.	Use compass points to give directions.
Prefer to read fiction—short stories and novels.	Prefer nonfiction—descriptions of real events, action, and how things work.
Have many friends if they bully and likely bully someone they know.	Have few friends if they bully and more likely not know the person they attack.
Need encouragement to build them up.	Need reality checks to make them reassess and to be challenged.

Compiled from Michael Gurian and Kathy Stevens, "With Boys and Girls in Mind," *Educational Leadership*, Nov. 2004; Leonard Sax, *Why Gender Matters* (New York: Broadway Books, 2005).

Daddy Bond: How to Love Your Son

The other day while I was at the computer, a sharp object poked into my back.

A little voice challenged me to a duel. "Choose your weapon!"

Turning around, I found my youngest son with his Tinker Toy swords. I grabbed one of the weapons and halfheartedly "fought" him. Then I went back to the computer.

Unsatisfied, the boy persisted. Finally, I bounced out of my chair and chased him toward the kitchen. Once he entered that room, I stopped and ran back through the living room to the other entrance. Cutting him off at that doorway, I hollered, "Charge!"

With a delighted shriek, he spun around to get away.

We played this game for twenty minutes—and I believe Zane could have kept it up for another hour or two. He drank it all in, the running, the yelling, the battles.

A bit later, I was pushing him on the tire swing. After twenty minutes, I started to go inside. But Zane would have none of that. To the trampoline!

He bounced on the big black canvas, and I grabbed for his ankles. Once I successfully held on to an ankle, and I lifted up so he went falling backwards on to the tramp. A big bounce on his back, and he rolled. I grabbed an arm. He squirmed, I twisted, and he bounced again.

Dad, if you want to convey your love to your little guy, take the time to engage in some age-appropriate, physical play.

Daddy Bond: How to Love Your Daughter

In addition to my three sons, I've also been blessed with three daughters. Girls are so much different! None of my girls had even a week full of destroying things, making messes, and challenging me to a duel with Tinker Toys.

Where the boys like to literally tackle me, the girls like to *figuratively* tackle me and pin me down for one-on-one daughter/dad time. Now, recall what I said about generalizations? Let me address exceptions and offer a caveat. Each one of my three daughters is unique. Our middle girl, Saige, is most certainly feminine, but she also has a powerful, competitive personality that rivals any boy's aggressiveness. She lives life with gusto and verve. She thinks fast, she moves fast. She doesn't do anything halfway.

I used to describe Saige as "a red Italian sports car, zooming down the road with the throttle stuck wide open!" Typically this is the kind of behavior and attitude a dad expects from a son, not a daughter. That said, I love this girl's style! Saige is a delightful young lady, now in her teens, and her spontaneity, exuberance, and energy are wonderful traits. Her full-on approach to life was apparent early on.

Some years ago I was wrestling with a few of the kids when Saige, then six, was wildly attempting to escape my tickling fingers. In the process of getting away this tiny little blonde-haired girl wriggled wildly—and promptly put her foot right to my face! It was quite a whack. I recoiled in pain, and became the proud owner of a beautiful black eye (my first since grade school). My dear daughter was sincerely sorry. Of course, the injury wasn't intentionally inflicted, but still, it was reminiscent of the type of physical pain her older brothers used to inflict on me. They used to hurt us all the time. In contrast, my other daughters don't have a dubious distinction like this: giving Dad a shiner. What happened?

Aren't all little girls supposed to be all sweet and dainty? In a word, no! Lest you misunderstand, in addition to her obvious zest for life, Saige is also full of the qualities that we usually associate with the feminine gender. There's a softer side to her. She likes emotional movies, loves to talk on the phone (seemingly for hours), and spends lots of time in front of the mirror—just like her sisters. And she still leans into me for hugs at night and leaves me little love notes—things my teen boys refused to do after they turned eleven or twelve (no surprise there).

So, here's a complex girl who defies stereotypes. If you have a daughter, you might be fortunate to have a Saige. Conversely, you might be blessed with a quiet, reserved, and delicate girl. Likely you have someone who is in between. Regardless, you are going to want to embrace God's design for your child and enjoy her fully!

When younger, one of my girls' favorite things to do with me was to play "pretend." "Pretend" for a little girl is often something rather sedate, and for many men, somewhat tedious. It usually involves a lot of preparation—get the table and teacups ready, build the "house" just right, be sure that the stuffed animals are all gathered.

After that, there's a lot of time together. Sitting. Conversing about small, mundane things. Role-playing. Being polite to each other. "Nurturing" the animals or dolls.

This is not exciting. You won't *want* to do this kind of pretend play. You'll want to interject some action, speed the pace up, make things more . . . interesting. Don't do that, though. Instead, adjust your expectations and style to meet your precious little girl right where she is. Go to her interests, her play interests, her way of relating.

You *can* do this! You did it with her mom. Surely in the courting process, and since you married, you've realized that your woman needs relational time, time to be together, time to talk. She wants you—not your noises, not your ability to arm wrestle or to destroy things. It is the same dynamic at work in your daughter's life. She relates to you differently than the guys, and you've got to work a little harder (okay, sometimes a whole lot harder!) to do that. Trust me, it is worth the effort.

I'll assure you that as she matures, you'll find loving your girl gets easier. As they've gotten older, my daughters have each loved going out for breakfast with Dad, usually at a local bagel joint, where we simply sit and talk. Our conversations—over time—have become deeper and more meaningful. I can see my girl lean forward and soak in whatever affirmation and affection I'm able to relay. This is the payoff for investing in their lives, in meaningful ways, from early on. It is the dividend for demonstrating my love in a way that they can relate to and appreciate.

So the bottom-line: Adjust your fathering according to your child. Meet him where he is. Pour into her life in a way that is meaningful to her. Recognize that each child is unique, that boys and girls tend to be quite different, and that you'll have to rise to the challenge and give this kid your best effort. I want you to understand that each child—yours included—has his or her own gifts, abilities, interests, and needs. He or she is special! It is imperative that you study and appreciate those distinctive traits.

And trust me, the time will pass quickly. If you do this well, you'll likely find some relational gold when that son or daughter is older!

Understanding the Implications of Attachment

My colleague Pete is a happy father of two young boys. He and his wife enjoy a strong marriage and complement the other in parenting. There is love in the home and each tries to lift the other up in the eye of their sons.

When little Max turned two, Pete began a tradition of

doing something special with him on the nights when Lori, his wife and Max's mom, was at choir practice. One night they might build a fire in the backyard and roast marshmallows. Another evening found them at the city pool, swimming under the stars.

What could possibly be wrong with this tradition? Nothing—except that once Max started talking in sentences he would occasionally say things like, "Mommy, is tonight choir? Are you leaving?" Or, on a day when a blizzard closed roads, little Max bellowed in frustration, "But I like it when you leave, Mommy!"

As a father, it's important to remember that it's perfectly normal to have a male son begin to bond with his daddy. In other words, a healthy boy will begin to pull away from his mother at around two or three and begin to resonate with his father. This should happen! However, don't forget that in the process, it's easy for Mommy's feelings to get hurt. At first, Pete thought it was neat that his son wanted to spend time with him, which it was, but he didn't take his wife's hurt feelings into consideration. Big mistake. Whatever you do as a father, make sure you regularly affirm and applaud your child's mother. Failure to do so will cause grief and tears on every level.

A Final Word

Dad, if you take nothing else away from this book, I hope you'll remember this: Despite the differences between genders and the need to personalize your parenting to effectively reach them, there is a common denominator. Your child is desperate for your time and attention. Whether it's chasing your son around the house or sitting on a tiny chair with your daughter at her tea table, more than half the challenge is simply being there and investing in him or her.

Give your children the time and they will respond and be on their way to becoming the persons God intended.

Enhancing Teaching and Parenting for Girls

- Use puzzles to foster perceptual and symbolic learning.
- Verbally encourage girls who exhibit low self-esteem or who underestimate their abilities.
- Promote physical activities that foster gross motor skills.
- Use manipulatives, especially in science and math.
- Provide role models of girls succeeding at activities or school subjects normally associated with boys.
- Provide opportunities for girls to study together.
- Expect girls to ask for help and want to affiliate with a teacher.
- Encourage girls to actively explore their world, even at the risk of failure or minor injury.
- Let girls create their own challenges in which they can take safe risks.
- Realize loud or repetitive noises may distract girls, since their hearing is more acute than most boys.
- Provide role-playing activities.
- Be aware of how much stress a girl is feeling, as it may degrade her performance.
- Use a supportive, nonconfrontational approach to change a girl's behavior. Smile and look a girl in the eye.
- Provide alternative ways for girls to relax, such as hiking, sports, meditation, and concerts.
- Don't transfer your authority to a child. Establish the prohibitive rule. Stick to it. Then offer an alternative activity.[10]

Enhancing Teaching and Parenting for Boys

- Use manipulatives that require boys to use fine motor skills.
- When possible, provide a larger learning space.
- Make lessons kinesthetic and experiential. Structure activities for movement.
- Keep verbal instructions short. Don't layer instructions. Write layered instructions as numbered steps on a board or worksheet.
- Many boys may not hear as well as girls and need to be moved closer to the front of a room.
- Boys in groups do stupid things. Begin any new physical activity with directions from a trained teacher.
- Boys learn the "rules of the game" through aggressive play. Competition builds camaraderie and organizes their peer relationships. Don't eliminate PE and other physical activities from the school day or boys' aggressive drive will show up elsewhere—inappropriately.
- When a boy wants to be alone, ask him about his life. Stress tends to cause boys to choose isolation.
- Avoid small-group activities unless each boy has a different but equal goal, yet all members are held responsible for a team score.
- Provide a moderate level of stress through timing or some sort of challenge to engage a boy's interest.
- Give clear and consistent discipline.
- Don't transfer your authority to a boy. Establish the prohibitive rule. Stick to it. Look him in the eye and tell him so. Then offer an alternative activity.[11]

Suggested Resources

*What a Daughter Needs from Her Dad: How a Man
    Prepares His Daughter for Life,* by Michael Farris
    (Bethany House).

*What a Difference a Daddy Makes: The Indelible Imprint
    a Dad Leaves on His Daughter's Life,* by Dr. Kevin
    Leman (Thomas Nelson).

*King Me: What Every Son Wants and Needs from His
    Father,* by Steve Farrar (Moody Publishers).

*Raising a Modern-day Knight: A Father's Role in Guiding
    His Son to Authentic Manhood,* by Robert Lewis
    (Tyndale House).

*Bringing Up Girls: Practical Advice and Encouragement
    for Those Shaping the Next Generation of Women,* by
    Dr. James Dobson (Tyndale House).

*Bringing Up Boys: Practical Advice and Encouragement
    for Those Shaping the Next Generation of Men,* by
    Dr. James Dobson (Tyndale House).

Chapter 9

Helping Your Child Succeed

If you want children to keep their feet on the ground,
put some responsibility on their shoulders.
—ABIGAIL VAN BUREN

DETERMINE A LONG-TERM strategy for
maximizing your impact as a father and your
child's success later in life. This chapter offers
help in determining the best things to consider—
like character, curiosity, and common sense.

D o you remember the popular movie trilogy from the 1980s
titled *Back to the Future?* The films starred Michael J. Fox as
seventeen-year-old Marty McFly, who rode backward and forward in time using a modified DeLorean. Just for fun let's take
Marty's time machine for a jaunt into the future.

Your seven-year-old boy, the firstborn apple of your eye, is
playing baseball in the city's parks and rec league. You've played
catch with him, gotten him a plastic bat and ball, and tried to
help him figure out the game's mechanics. You've encouraged
him for these past few years. You've tried to give him the tools
to succeed—at some level—at playing baseball. You want him
to do well. You want to help him avoid embarrassment.

Although it's difficult to admit, he isn't particularly gifted
as an athlete, and the game's finer points regularly elude him.
But here you are, at a game, watching him out in right field,
cheering him on.

As you sit high in the stands with the other parents, you
notice he seems to be daydreaming. He probably wouldn't
see a fly ball if one came his way.

Inside you try to get his attention. "C'mon, son, get your
head into the game. Be ready for the batter to hit it. And if you
do get the ball, where are you gonna throw it?" But he remains
distracted by the butterflies.

As you try to project your thoughts to him, you realize
that, at least for now, your boy isn't terribly interested in the
game. He's probably not going to be a superstar on this—or any
other team.

In fact, as he gets older, he's not likely to play any sport.

What do you do with that?

Something like this happened to me. I was the dad in the
bleachers waiting to see how my son might catch the ball. I
watched him struggle to enjoy the game, flinching when a ball

was hit his way. I tried, unsuccessfully, to interest him in sports. By the time he was ten, we'd given up on organized athletics. Despite my expectations, I finally had to admit my son wasn't very interested in sports. He wasn't competitive. He just didn't care about winning.

He preferred mechanical challenges (like disassembling a toaster) to the thrill of stealing a base or hitting a double. Organized sports didn't fit his personality.

What was I expecting? How important to me was my son's involvement in sports? Was success in athletics significant for his success in life?

It's not that we gave up at the first sign of disinterest in athletics. We tried a number of sports. But eventually it became apparent that this was a wasted effort. In the end, I learned to let go of my hopes that this boy would excel in sports—any sport.

Instead of chasing the dream of a son with great athletic prowess, I concentrated my parenting energies on the things that really matter, the things my wife and I value. I traded my hopes for vicarious sports stardom for a burning desire to infuse my son with the internal qualities that linger much longer than a summer league trophy.

Things like honesty, loyalty, integrity, compassion, and character.

Defining Success

While critical life qualities can be learned in sports, they can also be acquired through a number of other activities. It took me awhile to appreciate that, but it's been a liberating realization.

So, if parenting aims at helping our kids succeed in life, what's success going to look like for your firstborn?

Singer and songwriter Bob Dylan summed up success this way: "A person is a success," he said, if he "gets up in the morning and gets to bed at night and in between does what he wants to do."

Is he right? Is success just a matter of personal fulfillment? Or does it go deeper?

In sports, success usually has a clear definition. For professional teams, it's winning the Super Bowl, or the World Series, or for those more globally minded, the World Cup. For individuals, success means winning the Masters or Wimbledon, the Indy 500 or the Boston Marathon. For Olympic athletes, success means stepping onto the platform and accepting that gold, silver, or bronze medal.

The business world measures success in terms of shareholder value, company size, completing a project under budget, meeting a sales target, or gaining in market share.

In education, success means an improvement in test scores, winning the band competition, or attaining an advanced degree.

Most of us have a definition of success that we—consciously or unconsciously—strive for. It might be a title at work, a level of income, or a particular social status. We might identify our success by our friends, our accomplishments, or maybe even having specific character qualities.

Historical Perspective

One of George Washington's favorite theater performances was Joseph Addison's *Cato*. He saw it numerous times and even had it performed for his troops at Valley Forge. It has a line of dialogue that not only Washington but also John Adams regularly quoted:

Tis not in mortals to command success; but we'll do more
. . . we'll deserve it.

I wonder how many of us can appreciate this mind-set.
Most of us have been taught, perhaps subtly, that victory equals
success. The late George Steinbrenner, owner of the New York
Yankees, once said, "Winning is the most important thing in my
life, after breathing. Breathing first, winning next."

Based on his thirty-plus years as boss of the storied baseball franchise, George Steinbrenner wasn't kidding. For him,
victory trumped everything else.

What about your family? How will you measure success
in parenting your firstborn? How will you determine if your
child is succeeding?

Let me suggest that for you to prepare your new child for
success you need to first determine *what* success is—for your
child and for your parenting. Only then will you be able to
know how to help your child aim for the gold.

While you need to come up with your own definitions, let
me propose a few measures of parenting success—some things
quite different from the normal hallmarks.

Measurements

True success isn't a list of accomplishments. While making
the honor roll, being a star player, or selling the most cookies can
reflect good things in a child's life, taken at their face value
they're merely activities. Anyone can be busy, and these days it
seems that *outstanding* is a superlative almost any kid can attain.

As one school banner proclaimed, theirs is a facility "Where
every child succeeds." Really? How is that? Only by considering

external accomplishment can we ascribe "success" to everyone in a program.

There's something deeper to true success. Something more substantial. Something harder to achieve, harder to measure, but long-lasting and deeply meaningful. I'm talking about intangible but ultimately significant qualities. Things like character, compassion, curiosity, and common sense. These will truly make for a successful life. If my sons and daughters possess these traits, I'll consider them successful—and our parenting effective.

The Importance of Character

My wife asked our youngest daughter the other day, "What do you think character means?"

Tauvi replied, "It's who you are when no one is looking."

I think my daughter got it right. If my kids will make good choices and behave when no one is looking, they'll show some character.

Abraham Lincoln once said, "Reputation is the shadow. Character is the tree." Our character is not just what we try to display for others. Good character is doing the right thing because it is right.

Dictionary definitions of character usually reflect inner qualities like honesty, loyalty, courage, integrity, compassion, commitment, and devotion.

At times, circumstances reveal our child's previously hidden attributes. Difficult situations cause someone's true character to become apparent.

Here's how the US Air Force Academy defines character:

> . . . the sum of those qualities of moral excellence that stimulate a person to do the right thing, which is manifested

through right and proper actions despite internal or external pressures to the contrary.

Where does your child learn to acquire good character? The primary place is within your family. School, Scouts, and sports can help, but it is within your family that such attributes are cultivated and refined.

Let's look at a few aspects of character you may want your child to have as he grows up. You'll likely not see evidence of these for many years. So it helps to take a long view, think through the matter now, and plan to mold your child in the coming years with purpose.

The Power of Conviction

Having the courage of one's convictions is something I want for my children. They need to know what they believe, and why; they need to be able to defend those beliefs; and they need to let those beliefs define their life's activities.

I can recall as a freshman in college my first tastes of true freedom. Life was mine to define and live out three hundred miles from home. For all practical purposes, nobody would know what I did.

I watched as classmates engaged in heavy drinking and drug use. Despite their availability and the freedom I was experiencing, I declined the opportunity to drink alcohol or smoke marijuana. I knew such behaviors had negative effects, and while I don't recall my parents talking with me about the dangers of substance abuse, my deeply held beliefs about drugs and alcohol helped me avoid them. This isn't a dramatic story, but it illustrates one character quality: *conviction*.

Can Curiosity Be Taught?

In the 2009 remake of *Sherlock Holmes*, the lead character has an insatiable curiosity. It often leads him into dangerous situations, but it also enables Holmes to solve puzzling crimes. In one scene when a character dismisses "the small details" of a situation, Holmes counters that it is the small things that really bear consideration.

Holmes's curiosity set him apart. I suggest that a curious character will make for a lifelong learner—something that will set your child apart from his peers.

Passive ingestion of video games, movies, and online video seems to diminish a child's ability to think clearly and act creatively. We watch (and even encourage) our children to sit more and use less brain power.

Rather than accept passive entertainment, use the tools at your disposal (nature, the public library, car rides, and anything else you can think of) to challenge, equip, and encourage your child's healthy curiosity of the world and how it works.

Can Compassion Be Caught?

Real compassion means to care for those who are hurting, powerless, and needing assistance. It is definitely a quality I want to see in each of my kids. As they demonstrate other-centered hearts, they reflect the heart of God and reveal an inner quality this world desperately needs. And in so doing, they'll be truly successful.

To cultivate compassion, you've got to model it.

The trip was the realization of my wife's dream of a family service project. We traveled with two other families (our entourage included six adults and thirteen children).

We centered our activity on an orphanage in Ayacucho, Peru, where we spent most of our time loving on some precious children who had experienced a lot of difficulty in their short lives. These kids had no family, but they were a family, living together and developing bonds through their common pain.

It was gratifying to see my children interacting with the orphans. They instantly—and intuitively—knew that physical touch was important to the young residents of Casa Luz. They scooped up the littlest ones, hugging and holding them. When the older children came in from school, our kids engaged them in conversation, through some mangled Spanish and English translating, and some soccer on the patio.

Despite language and cultural differences, we watched our children reach out to kids who were disadvantaged in so many ways. Bonds were formed that remained in place long after we left Peru.

I was pleased that all our kids showed compassion. They looked out for and into the lives of the children we visited. They didn't consider themselves better than the orphans—they realized how privileged we are in America and how little those Casa Luz kids really had. This wasn't pity—merely feeling bad about someone else's situation—this was compassion at work. And it came from their hearts.

I'm convinced my children had hearts that cared for those fatherless kids. Probably part of that developed when we adopted our youngest child . . .

The "paper pregnancy" took about twenty months, and we spent a considerable time talking and praying about our reasons for adopting. We already had five biological children, so it wasn't like we couldn't have tried for another "flesh and blood" baby. Instead, Dena and I were moved to reach out to a child who had no realistic opportunity to have a reasonably normal life. After seeing the Russian orphanages and realizing our son was literally one in a million, we were convinced we made a good decision. We've wondered if we should pursue another adoption. Zane's special needs, however, have been significant, so we've ruled that option out.

The compassion we saw in our kids on that trip to Peru came out in some unexpected ways. The most touching was a week or two after we returned, when our eleven-year-old daughter announced to us that our family should expand. Reflecting on her recent experience at Casa Luz, Tauvi blurted out, "I think we should adopt Ezekiel."

"Excuse me," I said. "What did you say?"

"I think we should adopt Ezekiel, because he was cute, and I think he needs a family, too."

"Well, honey, that is sweet, and I hope you'll pray about that," I said. "We're pretty maxed out with Zane's needs and all the activities for the rest of you kids. But if God tells us to adopt, we will."

I had hoped my "pray about that" admonition would help Tauvi understand there's a lot to adoption (she was only five when her younger brother came into our family). A month or so later, I knew what was in her heart when a friend at church approached me.

"So, your family is expanding? That's exciting!"

"'Scuse me, Jeff?"

"When we take prayer requests in Sunday school class, your daughter prays for a boy in Peru named Ezekiel. So when are you bringing him home?"

"We're not convinced yet that we'll be adopting Ezekiel. But we are praying . . ."

I realized Tauvi's heart was truly full of compassion. And I can get a bit emotional as I think that she'd care enough to pray on a consistent basis (that's tough for middle-school kids), and that she'd be willing to give up some things to see Ezekiel become part of a "forever family."

That's compassion, and if my children see others and want to help, they're really successful in my eyes.

THE SUCCESS OF love is in the loving—it is not in the result of loving. Of course it is natural in love to want the best for the other person, but whether it turns out that way or not does not determine the value of what we have done.

—MOTHER TERESA

Building toward Character

If you feel overwhelmed as a first-time dad by the things we've considered in this chapter, relax. You've got a lot of time to build your child's character. There will be plenty of opportunities to teach and model the kind of character you want to see in your little boy or girl.

The process of imparting character to your child is organic—it isn't a program so much as an approach to life that involves living out your convictions and involving your child in your world. Live out your beliefs in such a way that your kid sees what's going on (kids pick up on almost everything)!

My friend James and his wife, Joan, live a life that is consistent, caring, and pretty remarkable. They invite needy individuals into their home for months at a time. They live without debt so they can contribute to Christian causes. In a world of conspicuous consumption, they buy secondhand. They sold most of what they had to serve in Scotland as missionaries.

James's children have learned firsthand about other cultures, living frugally, serving people, and being selfless—because they see their dad and mom choosing those values daily. His kids, now young adults, reflect their father's character because through the years they saw him modeling a set of deeply held beliefs. They're just practicing what he preaches and lives.

Sail On! Sail On!

Ferdinand Magellan was a Portuguese navigator who left his native land and petitioned Charles V and Cardinal Jimenez of Spain to commission him for a risky and bold expedition. Magellan suggested he would find a route to the Moluccas around the southern coast of America, instead of the usual, much longer route around the Cape of Good Hope.

The trip proved excruciatingly difficult. Many of those under his charge demanded they return to Spain. He held firm, assuring them of their coming success. The crew grew increasingly agitated. A mutiny seemed inevitable. For three months and twenty days, Magellan and his fleet sailed without sight of land. Provisions dwindled. He finally caught sight of the Ladrones, and just over a week later discovered the Philippines.

Writing in his book *The Call*, Os Guinness reflects on the remarkable incident:

Magellan was not tall, handsome, nor physically impressive in any way. He had no particular social status. Whatever advantages he might have lacked in one area or another, he made up for with one thing: He was a dreamer fired by an inner vision . . .

He faced many difficulties and failures, the types of circumstances that would have stopped lesser men. Whatever happened, Magellan's response was always, "Sail on, sail on!" He never flinched. It was always, "Sail on, sail on!" Magellan's character was far from perfect . . . but in his singlemindedness, his unflinching conviction, his resolute indifference either to approval or rejection, and his stubborn defiance of discouragement, defeat, and death, Magellan demonstrated the fortitude of a life in focus.[12]

This is a worthy theme for life: Regardless of the situations we face, let us, as fathers commissioned to help our children succeed, move with courage and conviction and "run the race set before us"!

Suggested Resources

Heroes Among Us, by Jim Ryun (Destiny Image).

Amazing Grace Audiobook, by Dave Arnold, Paul McCusker (Focus on the Family).

Books That Build Character: A Guide to Teaching Your Child Moral Values Through Stories, by William Kilpatrick (Simon & Schuster Trade).

Chapter 10

The Keys to Your Child's Heart

The great man is he who does
not lose his child's heart.
—MENCIUS, BOOK IV

EXTERNAL RULES CAN shape a child's behavior. But to be most effective as a new dad you'll want to give your kid a set of internal drivers to shape his or her heart. This chapter offers keys to keeping their attention—and affection—in the coming years.

We hadn't seen each other for some time, so I asked my friend "Mitch" how he was doing.

He said he'd been struggling at home with "the usual teen troubles."

One daughter was rebelling and dating someone against Mitch's wishes. Another was acting out, always arguing and fighting, and wanted to leave home despite being only sixteen. He didn't know how to handle his other two children, either. Mitch couldn't talk to the kids without arguing, they rarely obeyed him, and he couldn't understand why they didn't respect him.

Tough stuff, for even the most veteran parent.

To other adults, Mitch projected confidence as a dad. But inwardly he felt insecure in his parenting. The family was in conflict, and as Mitch shared his troubles, my heart grew heavy.

He wants to do well and has tried to be a good father. Mitch desperately longs to connect with his children and guide them to adulthood. He wants the best for his kids, but his teenagers were rejecting his advice and his role in their lives. By most measures, he was missing the mark.

A Soft Evaluation

Unfortunately, Mitch's difficulties were no shock to those who know him. He's always seemed to be searching for his own manhood, trying to prove his worth and establish his own importance. Mitch tends to do things that may bring him significance and acceptance.

Whether heading off to the mountains to hunt, spending a day helping a friend, or serving at church, Mitch had endless excuses about being away from his family. Many of those reasons were reasonable and even generous to others. Unfortunately his family paid the price. His absences were felt, and eventually the neglect caught up with him.

Either Mitch didn't see the needs in his own family, or he felt so inadequate on the home front that he escaped by being gone a lot. He seemed incapable of staying home to engage with his wife and children, especially while his kids were young. Other things always seemed to take precedence. Now, his kids' actions have become a reflection of his choices. They didn't sense a strong relationship with their dad, and they've rejected him.

Your Special Key

Imagine it's late and raining, and your wife arrives home with your new baby, maybe after a quick run to the store for some diapers and formula. You're working late, or maybe even out of town overnight on business. As your wife goes to open the door, she realizes (perhaps in her post-baby, sleep-deprived stupor) she's lost the key. She can't break a window, and there is no spare key under the mat or in the flowerpot. (That was your job, Dad, and you forgot.)

What can she do? She'll have to call a twenty-four-hour locksmith to let her in and make her a new key.

In many ways, being a father is like always making sure you have the key to the house. Every child's heart has a lock, and a father possesses a special key that will unlock it. Sadly, other people, like locksmiths, can gain access to it, but usually through tainted means. It might even be a predator or a boy with ulterior motives. Sometimes the lock remains closed and the heart grows cold. You, Dad, have been given a key to a great treasure—your child's heart! But you need to be there to use it.

Mitch is losing his family because he's been away so often, although he possesses the very thing that will save what now appears lost: the keys to his children's hearts.

Real Life, Real Problems

I know you're a new dad, and this real-life illustration may seem irrelevant to what you are currently dealing with. Here is where you likely are right now. You're an honest, faithful, and enthusiastic father who is trying mightily to balance your family with your work. But you find yourself (soon to be) contending with a crying baby, dirty diapers, and the clutter of an infant's stuff. This is what seems to define your world, and it is impossible to envision anything different.

I affirm what you already know. This is an all-consuming time for a parent. You are rightly concentrating your energies on learning how to care for your new baby. It's difficult to see your new little guy or gal as a teenager. But while this season in life seems never-ending, it will pass all too soon.

If you haven't yet had other parents tell you, let me break the news: Before your eyes, this child will grow up and leave your home . . . and you won't believe how fast it will happen. Trust me—this season of parenting will pass by impossibly fast.

This little bundle of joy will one day push away and seek independence. You'll have an emotional, hormone-laden teen who won't believe every word you say. They'll ask you to "prove it," they'll push the boundaries, and they'll make you weep.

While that remains many years in the distant future, what you do now—now!—will pave the way for relational success in your child's life. As Mitch found out, one day you'll have teens, and what you do today will influence how smoothly those years go.

You have the power to build a bridge to your child, and to keep the lines of communication open. This is your responsibility, not your child's. You have to establish a solid parent-child relationship, and some things you can do now will make the coming years much easier. You hold the key to your newborn's heart. Today you can begin using it to establish and grow the connection between you, and keep it strong.

> **A KEY TO YOUR child's heart can be summed up in this simple statement:** *Kids yearn for a relationship—with you.*

Time Equals Love

Children spell "love" differently than most adults. I have a reminder of that on a little sticky note I made years ago, and which I still keep in my desk drawer at work. They spell it T-I-M-E. Our children desperately crave our attention. I can think of many days when, as I was crunched for time and ran around the house to get things done, one of my little ones eagerly shadowed me. When I asked if they needed anything, the answer was almost always: "No, Daddy. I just want to be with you!"

So what's considered normal? How much time do most dads spend with their children?

A recent study by two economists at the University of California, San Diego, found that college-educated fathers spent, on average, 9.6 hours per week with their children. Men who didn't graduate from college reported being with their kids 6.8 hours. Prior to 1995, fathers were either more honest or less interested, with college grads spending 4.7 hours and other fathers spending 3.7 hours per week.

The Key to Your Child's Heart
by the Smalley Relationship Center

We're convinced it's possible—and not too complicated—to raise confident, responsible kids in a warm, close-knit family atmosphere. What is the relational heart of parenting? We believe there are four things involved with successful parenting of children ages 0 to 12:

1. Maintain a close, trusting relationship with your child.
2. Motivate children to do their best.
3. Preserve order and harmony at home and have fun in the process.
4. Equip kids for future careers, interests, and relationships.

A single essential principle can mean the difference between an angry, rebellious, distant child and a happy, cooperative one. The key to your child's heart is knowing how to keep your child's spirit open. This is a time-tested principle that allows your child to experience their full potential as children and adults.

We define an open spirit as keeping the anger out of your child's heart. We emotionally injure our children all the time; that is not the dangerous aspect of parenting. We cannot be perfect as parents. But what is damaging is allowing the anger to stay unattended in our child's heart. Opening our child's spirit entails several key ingredients. One ingredient is softness.

When we hurt our child's feelings, it is crucial we approach our child with softness and sensitivity to their feelings. We can often degrade our children's feelings because we are embarrassed, angry, or confused. Try to ignore these feelings and force ourselves to focus on our child's heart with softness. "Honey, I can't believe I said those words to you. I am so sorry for making you feel bad. Can you forgive me?" This is a great start in opening our children's heart when they are hurt or angry with us.

Adapted by permission from *The Key to Your Child's Heart*, by Dr. Gary Smalley (Nashville: Thomas Nelson, 2003).

Be a Student . . . of Your Child

If you expect an easy approach to raising your baby, this may disappoint you: There's no perfect way to parent. There's no shortcut to greatness. Although there is a *Parenting for Dummies* book put out by the "For Dummies" publishing empire, dads are wise to realize that since every child is unique, every child requires an individual plan.

So what can you do now to make sure you are the best dad to your baby? Let me suggest you study your child.

I know, I know . . . you're thinking, *What is there to study right now besides the faces she makes when she has gas or the way her head moves as she sleeps? There's not much to be done right now, is there?* That's right—to a point. What you *can* do today is begin to pay attention to your girl or boy's personality and become knowledgeable of the differences in temperament and internal makeup.

Traits of a Firstborn

One approach to understanding your child is to recognize the differences that birth order make in how he approaches life. At first most babies are the same, but after a year or two, you'll see some differences between your child and others.

You'll see this birth-order dynamic at work in any family you know—even among your own siblings. A firstborn child is wired differently than a second or third. This is true in my family. I'm the oldest of four kids, and we're all different—partly because of our own unique personalities and in part because of how we fit in the lineup of birth order. This is also something I can easily see at work in my own six children. The oldest is definitely different in makeup from the youngest—and every child in between!

Though it is still early in your parenting game, let me suggest you become acquainted with the excellent research and insights of Dr. Kevin Leman. While he has many helpful parenting books, check out especially his writings about birth order. As you likely have only one child (or one on the way), here are a few observations from Dr. Leman about what a firstborn child is usually like:

- perfectionist
- cautious
- apprehensive
- list-maker (Leman jokes that they make lists of their lists!)
- reliable
- well-organized
- conservative (not a risk taker)
- punctual
- serious
- scholarly
- dependable

While your baby won't show most of these firstborn traits for a few years, as he grows, you'll do well to remember these attributes and recognize the specialness of this little bundle. God has given him a unique personality—his role as a firstborn is part of the equation.

One Size Fits All?

"Foolish" is how I'd describe the person who tells you one size fits all when it comes to raising a child. You may not realize it, but you already know that's a bunch of hogwash. Think a moment about your siblings, the folks in your own family, or the people you know from work. Are any of them similar? Probably so. Are most of them different from you? Probably so! There's quite a range of personalities. Some people are natural leaders (or controllers); others are peacemakers. Some are detail-oriented and others are big-picture thinkers. Some kids take directions well; others reject any suggestion.

You may have heard the proverb, "Train up a child in the way he should go; even when he is old he will not depart from it" (Proverbs 22:6 ESV).

There's great wisdom in that, but here's what it isn't about: *Do everything just right and your child will never stray.*

There's no promise anyone can give you about how to impart guidance to a little boy or girl so he or she will always follow your directions. You can't expect a child to act a certain way—or to become a certain type of individual—just because you've done the proper things. There's no easy formula for projecting how a child will turn out.

So don't think that A + B = C. Kids don't read parenting books, so they won't know you have certain outcomes in mind with your parenting. You won't be able to track their projection just because you see a certain trend in their early years.

We thought our oldest son's interest in dismantling things, in how things work, and his aptitude in mechanics would lead to an engineering career. We also thought his hobby of drawing house plans and dabbling in architecture might be a predictor of a career in that field. But so far he's rejected any thoughts of becoming a mechanical engineer or a home-builder. Instead, through his college years he's developed a passion for history and teaching. The early predictors were wrong. We would have been foolish to push him into certain directions based on just those first years.

Personalize It

Now let's talk a bit about you. Yes, you. While you'll *want* to do everything right as a parent, you'll fail a lot. Simple things will trip you up. You'll get busy. You'll forget this little child has no idea they're irritating you. You'll yell. You'll find yourself apologizing for a lot of things.

One complication in your parenting journey is the fact that all involved parties are flawed. In addition to your child's propensity to mess up, you'll also make mistakes as you raise him. That makes it especially difficult to have any certainty about the results of your parenting.

"Kids will be kids," as another saying puts it. Eventually (probably sooner rather than later) your daughter will be pushing to make her own decisions and choose her own way of doing things. You'll cringe at her choices in clothing. You'll wonder what she could be thinking as she does *that* to her hair. And you'll find your influence diminishing as your child takes her cues more from friends than from you. When that happens, it's too late to make any significant course corrections. Your parenting is in a seismic shift, and there's no turning back—your relationship with that child will forever be changed.

Between your own shortcomings and failures and your child's tendency to grow up and take on responsibility for his or her actions, you'll be unable to guarantee anything—especially in those teen years. No "one thing" you do today will ensure your son or daughter will be happy and obedient tomorrow.

Train Up a Child

So what *is* the significance of the "train up a child . . ." verse? I've heard more than one expert suggest the key lies in these words: "in the way he should go." There are several interpretations to that phrase, but the one that seems most reasonable to me conveys a sense of "in the way he is designed," or "in the way he is wired."

If that's the case, a wise parent will be a student of their child, observing and identifying his unique personality. Then, Dad, you'll adapt your parenting approach to his inner makeup. So a loose paraphrase of this proverb might be:

> Consider your child's unique personality and temperament, then parent accordingly. Grab and shape his heart . . . and he will (eventually) do well in life, because you've trained him well.

To do that, you'll need to really know your child, reaching into their life and heart so you might shape them at their very core.

It Ain't Rocket Science

The good news about reaching your child's heart is this: *It doesn't take a rocket scientist's brains or knowledge to do this right.* There's no college degree or job experience you need to acquire to grab hold of her heart . . . for life.

This isn't overly complicated. In fact, the process of unlocking your child's heart is pretty simple. Be careful though. While it's simple, I'm not suggesting it's easy.

Truth is: You're now a dad. And there's a lot to parenting well. Most of it boils down to humility, hard work, and time.

When it comes to dealing with your child's heart, here are three practical tips for making the connection with your kid:

1. Time
2. Time
3. Time

No, that's not a typo. The most significant thing you can do in your child's life—the very best thing to do now—is to invest time. Lots of it.

Sedentary Parenting

But, you say, there's nothing to really *do*! This baby just sits around. Lies around, really. She doesn't talk. She sleeps a lot. She eats. Cries, too. She doesn't look at me much. What am I supposed to do?

Glad you asked. This is the part where you want to watch Mom. She gets this baby stuff, and chances are she intuitively understands what a baby needs: time holding, talking with, looking at, and being cared for by a loving parent.

So, Dad, slow down and drink in the wonderful gift that God gave you in this little bundle. Do some things that probably seem a bit unnatural, and even counterintuitive.

Sit in the rocker and hold that precious baby. Look in her eyes and make some contact. Sing to her. Read books—even though she doesn't seem to understand or care. Find ways to make her laugh. Enjoy the wonderful, otherworldly joy of holding a happy, sleepy baby against your shoulder as she goes to sleep. Listen to that contented in-and-out breathing . . . and the occasional sigh. Find the joy in this child, and hold on to the moment.

And let me suggest you also spend time praying for your baby. And for your own wisdom and discernment as a parent.

A Long Day's Night

Our oldest had some sleep issues for the first year or two, so we had a lot of long nights. One of my fondest memories of time with Dakota, just as a baby, involves our bedtime routine. After a new diaper and pajamas, Mom would feed him, then I'd take over. We'd head to the rocker, and I'd hold Dakota against my shoulder. I'd sing to him (*Amazing Grace* was a recurring fave). I'd talk to him. I'd hug him. I'd pray for him. And eventually . . . after an hour or two, he'd fall asleep.

You might question the benefits of such uninterrupted time with a baby. So did I! There are times, however, when I wish those days were back . . . not that I don't love having a good conversation about history, politics, or computers with him now that he's an adult. The simple joys of holding and loving a helpless baby are priceless.

Picture your new baby as having a piggy bank. It's the old-fashioned kind, about five inches tall, pink porcelain, with a slot on top for coins. When you spend some time with that child, you're depositing a dime or a quarter into that slot. Holding Junior while you sit on the porch? That's ten cents deposited. Singing a little ditty to her while you change her diaper? Another 25 cents into the bank. Playing hide-and-seek in the morning? Good job—and another quarter into the pig.

The interactions don't have to be huge, emotional exchanges. Instead, the continual input from you is adding up. Day after day, month after month, year after year, those deposits multiply. That investment may not seem so significant today, but in several years your child will have learned that you love her, that you like being around her, and that you are worth listening to. She's paying attention to your emotional deposits—even at this young age—and believe me, the effort will reap benefits over time.

And there *are* tangible benefits to your child when you cuddle, even though you may not see anything happening.

Scientific research has confirmed that parent-child bonding, or time together, helps parents attach to their child, and vice versa. Children who have successfully bonded will have a greater sense of security, will be less anxious, calmer, sleep more efficiently, develop better self-esteem, and form better friendships later in life.

Pay It Forward

If you show an interest in your child when he is young, he will naturally continue to seek a relationship with you when he grows older. If you invest your meaningful time, you'll reap a reward. And those benefits extend way past the immediate. The work you put into your youngster today will help pave the way for a good relationship when he or she hits the turbulent teen years and beyond.

There's no guarantee that spending time and loving on this baby will ensure a trouble-free adolescence. Nor will it protect you from heartache and difficulty with an older child. There's plenty of evidence, though, that being an involved dad, working to make emotional connections and making your child a priority, will help your child (and you) now and in the future.

Consider these beginning years as a time to "pay it forward." Investments in your child's life now will come back to you in wonderful ways. But remember, love is not something that gets paid back—it's something that will wonderfully re-emerge in various forms through the years.

Back to Mitch

Remember my friend Mitch?

He spent an inordinate amount of time away from the home. When his kids were younger, they rarely had that fatherly attention that could unlock their heart. They learned to "do life" without Dad. He didn't intentionally invest in their lives, so they navigated life without him. While their hearts were hungry for his input, he didn't give it to them in a way they found meaningful. As a result, when they hit the teen years they had no significant relationship with Mitch. It was, for all practical purposes, too late for Mitch to reach into their lives and unlock their hearts.

The most challenging time in life is the teen years. If an adolescent has to deal with the difficulties of friends, self-identity, and self-doubt without the affirmation of dad, they're likely to make bad choices.

Josh McDowell said something that Mitch's parenting challenges seem to have proven true: "Rules without relationship lead to rebellion."

I saw Mitch trying desperately to guide his teens. He was imposing boundaries and establishing rules—as he should have done earlier—without the benefits of the emotional deposits his children had desperately needed. He was enforcing rules but not providing any relational basis for doing so. While it wasn't apparent when his children were toddlers and in grade school, Mitch's approach to parenting resulted in teens who rejected parental rules and sought out relationships with others.

That was painful to watch.

I hope I've been able to show you how important your time, effort, and energy is in the life of your child. The golf can wait. Work is necessary, of course, but all in its proper place and proportion. The hours and days you invest in your child will never be wasted.

Suggested Resources
Books:

> *The Key to Your Child's Heart: Raise Motivated, Obedient, and Loving Children,* by Dr. Gary Smalley (Thomas Nelson).

She Calls Me Daddy: Seven Things Every Man Needs to Know about Building a Complete Daughter, by Robert Wolgemuth (Tyndale House).

The Birth Order Book: Why You Are the Way You Are, by Dr. Kevin Leman (Revell).

The Firstborn Advantage: Making Your Birth Order Work for You, by Dr. Kevin Leman (Revell).

Chapter 11

Spiritual Formation

You shall teach them diligently to your
children, and shall talk of them when you sit
in your house, and when you walk by the way,
and when you lie down, and you rise.

—DEUTERONOMY 6:7 ESV

FACING THE REALITY that many kids reject
or stray from their parents' spiritual values, this
chapter looks at why your child needs you to
lead the way in this crucial aspect of life—and
how a new dad can model healthy spirituality.

Maria was only four when she asked her mom about a song she learned at her Christian preschool. "Mommy, is it true that God has a big house in heaven?"

"Yes, sweetie," Mom replied.

"Are there lots of rooms there?" Maria asked.

"Uh huh, there are," Mom affirmed.

Mom realized Maria had learned "My Father's House," a song about heaven by the Christian group Audio Adrenaline.

"And we can play football there?" Maria asked.

Smiling, her mom said, "Yes, of course!"

"Mommy, how can I go to that house? I wanna go there."

Mary Beth and her husband, Steven Curtis Chapman, helped their little daughter understand how she could know God and have the assurance of going to heaven one day.

The Chapmans rejoiced in Maria's embrace of their faith. They couldn't have imagined that only a few months later they'd be saying good-bye to Maria—who died after a tragic accident. Despite the ache in their souls, they found consolation in knowing there would, one day, be a reunion with their daughter who is now enjoying the "mansion of glory" she had learned about.

Maria's story illustrates the power you have to help your child grab on to spiritual truths—and the urgency of spiritual training in the home. It's never too early to introduce your child to faith . . . although if you put such training off, it could be too late.

Faith and Family

I'm a follower of Christ, and my relationship with God is my life's priority. As a Christian parent, my ultimate goal in raising my children has been to introduce them to God and to help them to know and understand Him.

Let me be clear: I want well-behaved kids. I want children who are good thinkers, who have inner character, and who will eventually become men and women of integrity and compassion. I want my children to turn out well.

But more than those qualities, more than anything, I want them to know my God and to live a life of faith. I'll do what it takes to help them understand and know God. There's an urgency to do that early, often, and, especially, in the home.

Edith Schaeffer, in her book *What Is a Family?*, observed that the family is where principles are established in the midst of everyday life, where character is forged under the watchful eyes of caring parents, and most important, where the baton of faith is passed to the next generation.

In the context of the everyday, through the rhythms of life's joys and disappointments, your child will see your faith. He will notice how you handle difficulties. She will observe the way you react to pressure.

Your belief in God is most effectively "caught, not taught" within the relationships and safety of family. Your child will, whether you like it or not, tend to imitate your priorities in life—including the importance of your personal faith.

Like little Maria Chapman, the vast majority of those who come to faith in Christ do so when they are youngsters in the home.

No doubt, Maria saw her parents following God. And as she learned in the home, and in that preschool, their God was worth following. Like Steven and Mary Beth, you can and should model a life of faith that will influence your son or daughter's spiritual choices.

Exerting your spiritual influence now, while your child is young, seems to be crucial. According to a 2003 study by Barna Research, "If a person does not accept Christ as Savior before the age of fourteen the likelihood of ever doing so is slim."

David Kinnaman, president of the Barna Group, reports his research has found that kids who received spiritual training are far more likely to remain actively engaged in their faith as an adult. "The odds of one sticking with faith over a lifetime are enhanced in a positive direction by spiritual activity under the age of eighteen. And it [our study] raises the intriguing possibility that being involved at least a few times a month is correlated with nearly the same sticking power as weekly involvement—especially among teenagers."[13]

Now—not later—is when you have to think through and start taking action for the benefit of your child's faith.

Don't Wait

I recall being impressed by Gerry as I sat beside him on a plane. He was in his thirties, married with one young child and another on the way. As we talked, I asked him about his own experiences and the needs of the other guys in his home fellowship.

His answer didn't come as a surprise. He said that spiritual leadership is a major concern to him. His dad didn't model it. So while Gerry knows he needs to lead well in his home, he doesn't really know how to do that.

I did my best to encourage him, just one Christian father to the next. But the exchange got me thinking: *This is not an isolated incident. Chris is representative of millions of Christian dads who truly want what is best for their children . . . but feel woefully unprepared to teach them about the most important thing of all.*

The River of Culture

In speaking to a roomful of concerned parents, radio host, author, and mom Janet Parshall told them that the responsibility to train their children is theirs. Theirs alone. "If you don't work to pass along your values to your children," Parshall said, "the culture will do it for you."

She's right. You have to own your child's spiritual formation. If you don't invest in your little one's spiritual values, that void will be filled by others.

Most parents recognize the primacy of their responsibility and influence on the spiritual formation of their child. In that 2003 Barna study, almost 90 percent of parents said they believe they have the primary responsibility for teaching their children about spiritual matters, with 96 percent saying they are primarily responsible to teach their kids good values.

If you haven't yet considered that you are the primary shaper of your child's thinking and decisions about God, I urge you to think the matter through and to use your power wisely.

Your Spiritual Influence

Here's how my friend and former colleague Dr. James Dobson described in his book *Solid Answers* a mother's and father's responsibility in shaping faith:

Shortly after [a gosling] hatches from his shell he becomes attached, or "imprinted," to the first thing he sees moving near him—ordinarily the mother goose, on hand to hatch the new generation. The gosling is vulnerable to imprinting for only a few seconds after he hatches; if that opportunity is lost, it can't be regained later.

There's also a critical period in the life of children when concepts of right and wrong are formulated and views of God begin to solidify. The opportunity must be seized while available. Parents who withhold indoctrination from their small children, allowing them to "decide for themselves," almost guarantee that their youngsters will "decide" in the negative. Parents who want their kids to have a meaningful faith must give up misguided attempts at objectivity.

After about age fifteen, children sometimes resent heavy-handedness about anything—including what to believe. But if the early exposure has been properly conducted, they have an anchor to steady them.[14]

Science Confirms It Again

Social science supports that view of your role in your child's faith—and the findings emphasize the significance of parents in passing along faith. In the area of spiritual formation that lasts a lifetime, Dad and Mom are more influential than anyone or anything else.

Researcher Christian Smith studied the traits of religious American teenagers who retain a high faith commitment as emerging adults. His findings indicate that with regard to sharing our faith, the most important factor is parents. For better or worse, parents are tremendously important in shaping their children's faith trajectories. Looking down the road at your child's decisions about spirituality, it is clear that you hold the power of shaping a lasting faith in your newborn's life.

Dad, if you have a personal faith, it is your responsibility to help your child know your God. Nobody else will do it for you. Of course, your wife will likely share your faith, and she will be part of that spiritual training. Still, you've got to take the lead.

Building your child's spiritual foundation takes time and effort, but the effort is certainly worthwhile.

Being Purposeful in Faith Training

Let me suggest a passage from the Old Testament as a starting point in equipping your kids with a vibrant faith. It drives home the point that parents *must* be intentional, active, and relentless in the spiritual training of our children.

These commandments that I give you today are to be upon your hearts. Impress them on your children. Talk about them when you sit at home and when you walk along the road, when you lie down and when you get up. (Deuteronomy 6:6–7)

These Scriptures suggest that as a parent you have an obligation to:

- Believe personally and passionately in God (upon your heart).
- Talk about God with your children, in natural ways, consistently (impress on your children).
- Talk about your faith in the home (not leaving that responsibility to Sunday school teachers).
- Teach the truths of faith during the activities of your life (while sitting, walking, getting ready for bed, and arising in the morning).

Faith is something that starts in the heart. Of course, you must have a passion to follow God yourself—without that, you have nothing to offer your kids spiritually. We can't pass along what we don't already have.

These verses also speak of an element of purposefulness. The transmission of faith isn't something we can leave to chance. It's not an optional exercise or something we can do when there's time. Instead, we're told to weave our faith into our everyday lives—naturally, consistently, and intentionally.

You're not to leave this important matter to chance. You're to be purposeful and consistent in training your child.

In this day and age of tolerance and subjectivity, this kind of faith-teaching strikes some as heavy-handed. Some parents don't want to "force religion" on their children, preferring to let the kids discover their own spiritual path. But remember what Dr. Dobson suggested:

> Parents who withhold indoctrination from their small children, allowing them to "decide for themselves," almost guarantee that their youngsters will "decide" in the negative. Parents who want their kids to have a meaningful faith must give up misguided attempts at objectivity.

The words of Deuteronomy say we're to guide our kids to an understanding of God and His way of doing life. We aren't to let spiritual training "just happen," nor are we to let kids decide for themselves (or have another "decide" for them) what truth is. We're to shoulder the burden, step up to the responsibility, and do so with intentionality. And we're to do that naturally—in the context of ordinary life rhythms.

In addition to spiritual instruction, Dad, you also need to model a real faith. Show your love for Christ in your daily life. Be passionate about God. Demonstrate a love for Him, for His kingdom, for His Word. Your child will observe your heart and life—and will likely seek to emulate your faith walk.

Your passion for Jesus is something you can pass along to your child. That is the most important thing you can do in your son's or daughter's life. Pass the baton smoothly, and the foundation is laid for a family of faith that lasts for generations. After helping your child grab on to your faith, perhaps the next most important job is to give him a biblical perspective on life.

Pass Along a Biblical Perspective

If you see life through a lens of faith, you'll have a certain understanding of pain and suffering, of joy, work, community, finances, and morals.

Those with a different worldview may be motivated to live in ways that conflict with your beliefs. Despite your influence in your son's life, as he ages, his ear for your wisdom will diminish. Friends at school, philosophies he catches in movies and television, and the general tone of the culture will increase in significance.

In just a few short years ,when your boy begins school, the worldview you've taught will have increasing importance. By then I hope you've established a good foundation for filtering life. His worldview will shape his thinking, perception of truth, and behavior.

The world doesn't support a Judeo-Christian perspective of life. Instead, pop culture will tell your kids:

- You are the most important person; you are Number One.
- Nothing should get in the way of your pursuit of pleasure and fulfillment. Remember, it's all about you.
- Life is about whatever you want it to be . . . or it is worth nothing, if you'd like. You choose!
- There are no absolutes; there is no moral order to the world. Objective truth is a fairy tale, and it is up to you to define reality and truth—just for you, though, not for me.

A 2002 Barna survey of the general population asked people if they believe there are moral absolutes that are unchanging, or that moral truth is relative to circumstances. By a three-to-one margin, adults said truth is always relative to the person and their situation.

Such a perspective was even more predominant among teenagers. Eighty-three percent said moral truth depends on the circumstances, and only 6 percent said moral truth is absolute.

Unfortunately, this lack of moral clarity extends into the church. Half of those who call themselves "followers of Christ" don't believe the Bible is the true and infallible Word of God. They're relying on their own good sense or intuition to determine what is truth. There's an obvious disconnect between their stated beliefs and the foundation of that faith.

Chuck Colson of Prison Fellowship and Breakpoint.org cited his concerns about this dearth of conviction affecting Christian families, saying there is:

. . . a growing and disturbing evangelical disease: worldview blindness. This blindness is a direct result of people compartmentalizing their faith. Christianity is simply one of many compartments in their lives. The solution is teaching believers to see Christianity as an integrated life system, an explanation for all of reality. And then we must make worldview training an urgent priority for our kids, because they will have their faith challenged . . . on television, at the movies, by their friends—just about everywhere they turn. We need to reach these kids while they're young and impressionable—before the world has taught them to become skeptics.[15]

If you want a child with an internal moral compass, who lives with a clear understanding of right and wrong and with a personal knowledge of God, you've got to start early, be intentional, and be consistent in spiritual training.

Intentional Training: What You Can Do

If you have a passion for God, how can you help pass along your faith to your child? What does purposeful spiritual training look like? Apart from living an authentic life of faith, let me share some practical suggestions you can begin to adopt in your home with your family.

1. Read Bible stories to your child.

There are some excellent illustrated Bible story books for kids. Find a few different age-appropriate books to keep on hand and to read at bedtime or during quiet moments. Reading even one story every day, starting when that child is just a year or two old, can help foster an appreciation for Scripture and an understanding of God's heart and character.

Suggested starting points:

The Bible in Pictures for Toddlers, by Ella K. Lindvall (Moody Publishers).

The New Bible in Pictures for Little Eyes, by Kenneth N. Taylor (Moody Publishers).

Read Aloud Bible Stories: Volumes 1–4, by Ella K. Lindvall (Moody Publishers).

2. Have family devotions.

Even if your daughter is only a few months old, it isn't too soon to begin having a regular time of spiritual training for the family. Begin now so you feel comfortable and knowledgeable when she is older.

Many families include Bible reading in their postdinner routine, while others have a weekly time of spiritual engagement with their kids. Regardless how you go about it, be consistent and enthusiastic. Lead with some energy, and your child will more readily follow.

Suggested starting points:

It Starts at Home: A Practical Guide to Nurturing Lifelong Faith, by Kurt Bruner and Steve Stroope (Moody Publishers).

One Year of Dinner Table Devotions and Discussion Starters, by Nancy Guthrie (Tyndale House)

3. Pray.

Pray at meals, bedtime, in the morning . . . and when your child has an "owwie." Pray for your child. Pray with your child. Pray for your wife, as both a spouse and a mom.

Use the *Book of Common Prayer,* use a church prayer guide, make up prayers on the spot. The form of your prayer doesn't matter, so much as the practice of prayer.

The important thing is to consistently integrate prayer into your life. Don't reserve prayer for mealtime, reciting some rote "blessing" without meaning.

Suggested starting points:

A Journey to Victorious Praying, by Bill Thrasher (Moody Publishers).

How to Pray, by R. A. Torrey (Moody Publishers).

4. Attend church.

I know of parents who attend church merely "for the benefit of the kids." Dad and mom don't particularly want to be there, but they go to services because they see a value for their children. While that might strike you as a laudable sacrifice, to me it seems hypocritical. If those parents don't care to cultivate their own spiritual life, why should they think their kids will see church as anything more than an obligation to endure?

Instead, we ought to show our kids a vibrant and active life of involvement in a church community. Find a Bible-believing church that suits your tastes, one with a sense of community, and get involved. Find ways to serve. Look for ways that you— and your child—can help others. Demonstrate a commitment to a body of believers, and let your child see you (and, ideally, accompany you) in active engagement at a local church.

5. Play wholesome music in your home.

Even young children are sensitive to tone and can pick up on lyrics. One prominent musician quit his successful band after hearing his young daughter sing a song with lewd lyrics. She had been listening to *his* band's music, and the raunchy words entered her mind. Though she didn't yet understand the meaning of the lyrics, he was—rightly—appalled at what came out of her mouth. He felt such conviction that he decided to stop playing such music.

There is an abundance of good kids music with Christ-centered lyrics, available for you to play for your child.

Consider the music Maria Chapman was learning in pre-school, and the impact on her eternal destiny from that one song about heaven.

For a Christian parent, passing along a spiritual heritage is an all-important task. Nothing compares with its importance. What else can you do on a daily basis that carries with it such eternal consequences?

Dads, I urge you. Take the time. Find the time. Make the time. Tell your son or daughter about the greatest man who ever lived. Tell them about Jesus Christ.

Suggested Resources

Choosing to See: A Journey of Struggle & Hope, by Mary
    Beth Chapman (Revel).
Parents' Guide to the Spiritual Growth of Their Children,
    edited by John Trent, Rick Osborne (Tyndale
    House).
Teaching Your Child How to Pray, by Rick Osborne
    (Moody Publishers).
*The Power of Teachable Moments: Using Everyday
    Experiences to Teach Your Child about God,* by Jim
    Weidmann and Marianne Hering (Revel).

Chapter 12

Blink

Children are not casual guests in our home.
They have been loaned to us temporarily for
the purpose of loving them and instilling a
foundation on which their future lives will be built.
—DR. JAMES C. DOBSON

WHILE IT SEEMS impossible at the moment,
the cliché "blink and she'll be gone" will be true
in your fathering. In this chapter we'll discuss
what you need to know as you embark on a
lifelong parenting adventure and how to grow
a close relationship that will endure.

In late July 1991, I was pondering a job change. I was happy with managing two Christian radio stations in Texas. Our circumstances were close to ideal. We lived two blocks from my wife's sister and her family. One set of grandparents—we had one child at the time—lived only twenty minutes away. We belonged to a good church, had some wonderful friends, and loved our neighborhood.

To accept the new job would mean moving to Colorado and leaving all we had known as a young family. There'd be some tears if we took on the challenge of a new job in a new city and state. That was a lot of upheaval to consider.

As a complicating factor, we were expecting at any time the birth of a second child.

Weighing the opportunity, we sought counsel from trusted friends. After considerable prayer and thought, we decided to go for it.

Within hours of making the decision, Dena went into labor. In fact, Seth was born just eight hours after I called to accept the offer to join the Focus on the Family broadcast team. Six weeks later, I was in Colorado starting the new job.

Times, They Are Changing

I've now been with the organization for nearly two decades. The time has flown! One marker of our lives in Colorado Springs has been that child. I've gauged my tenure by Seth's physical growth. When we moved here, he was a tiny infant. Over the years he's grown quite a bit—he now stands six foot eight inches!

Blink.

I have vivid memories of his arrival here in Colorado, of that first Christmas here with no other family members nearby, of the fun times we enjoyed. I played with the two boys in a life-size replica they made of the *Dawn Treader* ship. Rowdy games of hide-and-seek in the evenings. Hours reading books, playing board games, going to the nearby park, practicing baseball, going on bike rides. As Seth got older, there were hunting trips, adventure in the mountains, and trips overseas. So many wonderful times with this boy!

Blink.

As my mind goes back through the years, I struggle to realize that the little baby with whom we moved here is now an adult, off on his own. Those past years are now lived out only in my mind, or when I look at photos that capture memories of time gone by.

I can't stop by his room to ask him a question. He doesn't eat dinner with us, then keep us at the table, entertaining us with his goofy sense of humor. No more late night conversations. No more hunting trips—for now. He's off on his own.

Blink.

All those sleepless nights, trips to the ER, times of shaping his character, praying with and for him, hours spent at the gym watching basketball games . . . now they're all just memories. In the past. My hard work that helped this kid grow up and become a man is over.

This present stage of parenting is much different from anything in the prior twenty years. And since we've launched two kids into adulthood, I think I can speak a bit about the value of having perspective—long-term perspective.

Look Where You Are Going

Right now, as a first-time dad, you have your hands full just caring for this newborn.

She didn't come with an owner's manual. She is a bundle of delicate baby-ness. She doesn't communicate clearly. She can't help you understand what she needs, so you're guessing a lot. You lack confidence about the coming years, thinking this is going to be a lot of work, and wondering what you can do to guarantee some level of success as a parent. You're learning to live on less sleep and more coffee.

Your relationship with your wife has been taking twists and turns as this bundle of joy requires most of her energy. And it seems this new normal will define the rest of your life.

This is not how your next twenty or thirty years will go. This is a season. Things will change! There will come a day when you watch your precious child walking away from your home. She'll become an adult. She'll leave for college. She'll walk down the aisle to become a wife.

Your role as a parent will change. You will leave the tasks of being the authority and helping your child learn about life— and instead become a friend. Your effort to guide your son to maturity, to cultivate in him a good heart, to equip him with the best tools for success, to enable him to find his place, will become but a memory.

Blink.

None of us can look into the future and see the result of our parenting efforts. If you just got home from the hospital with your newborn, you're starting a long—yet fast—journey.

There is no way to predict where that road called parenting will take you, nor to know with any certainty what that cute little bundle will be like in two decades.

Perhaps when you finish the parenting process, at least the first part, when you prepare your child for adulthood, you'll sit down and thank God for how well it all went. You'll be happy with the way your son turned out.

Or it could be you'll fall down in frustration and ask God what happened, wondering why your daughter rejected all you did and made such a mess of her young life . . . and asking if she will be able to salvage it.

Blink.

You may not realize this yet, but dads and moms are ultimately not responsible for the result of their parenting. You can't own the outcome. That grown child will be an individual on his own, free to make decisions, bad or good, to accept or reject the training you have instilled.

Your role as parent is to prepare the way, and then to allow your child to walk in it. Or not. You aren't entrusted to force your child to live life the proper way, only to show that son or daughter the best way to approach life.

The truth is, you probably won't live to see how that child finishes out their life.

I'm not trying to be fatalistic or negative. Parenting is wonderful! I hope you've caught that as you've read this book. There's so much to celebrate when raising a child. The wonderful memories, the times of laughter and fun, the satisfaction of a new skill learned, the moments of just being together . . . it is all good!

But there are many unknowns, and that includes the "end"—which often isn't when that boy turns eighteen and leaves home. "Boomerang kids" are increasing in number. Those adults who leave home—then return—often need parenting that is much harder than the kind you're about to start dealing with.

I've rounded that parenting corner and found there are changes you'll need to navigate. Let me briefly offer some dos and don'ts as you take the long view of being a dad.

How to Reap "Daddy Dividends"

The following journal entry, made when my oldest daughter was eleven, recounts a special day in which I felt particularly effective as a dad. It reminds me of the joys that accompany parenting, and I think it might help you, too.

As you read this entry, keep in mind that it included several moments of "intentional parenting," as well as some opportunities I was fortunate enough to see and take advantage of.

Yesterday was a day to spend time with my oldest daughter. It wasn't planned that way, but it turned out to be time well spent.

We started with our weekly "bagel and Bible" time, in which we head to a local shop and have some breakfast. Along the way, we open the Scriptures and interact about a particular passage. Yesterday was a hard one—Lamentations. All of it. The "weeping prophet" needed some contextualization for an eleven-year-old, and I think it was a meaningful conversation for both of us. I benefited from the reminder of right living and God's forgiveness.

Several hours later, I ended up being the driver to pick her up from an after-church event. That made for a nice drive home, in which we discussed the activities and people involved.

Midafternoon found us headed on another errand. Casual, a little chit-chat time for us.

Late afternoon she called when I was at the grocery store, and asked me to bring home some Cheerios for a dessert recipe she had started. This was a treat to take on a trip. Dutifully, I grabbed a box. Not an overly meaningful exchange, but I helped her out in a small way.

All in all, a number of little interactions with a girl who still looks up to me and values my attentions.

So . . . this morning. As I head out the door, on my desk I find a small item, wrapped carefully in foil, with a note. It was a nice little gesture. And it reminded me that the payoff was not just today, in getting a sweet treat from my daughter. The payoff really was yesterday. Time invested wisely. Not always overly purposeful. Didn't have to be. The point for my adolescent daughter was that she spent time with her daddy. And that I cared enough to be there for the little rhythms of life. I had made time to be with her.

Her note was simple and to the point. And it made me tear up.

"To my father who loves me."

What a welcome reminder . . . of the power God has given me as a daddy.

As I read that note years later, I get a lump in my throat. That daughter is now a vibrant sixteen-year-old. I'm happy to report I still have her heart . . . she still looks up to me, and she's still open to my fatherly guidance. I'm a fortunate man!

Here's hoping I make good use of that "daddy power" today in her life, and in the lives of my other children.

I want you to have that type of experience and impact on your child. That's why I've carved out the time to put this message down on paper. So often, too often, I cross paths with men who repeat the same phrase over and over. It's normally composed of two words:

If only.

If only they knew then what they know now. *If only* they worked less and stayed home more. *If only* they had made their children a priority and skipped playing in that softball league. *If only* they had realized how precious this time was.

A Month of Ways to Invest in Your Child's Life

Here are thirty-one ideas about how to invest in your relationship with your new child. As you do things together, you build bridges that will be wonderfully helpful—and enjoyable—in the years to come. You can begin to do some of these suggestions right now, others in a few years. I've done all these—enjoying some more than others, and finding each of my kids had preferences I needed to be aware of. After reading, add some ideas of your own!

1. Go out for breakfast.
2. Sing a song to your child when you change a diaper.
3. Take a bike ride together.
4. Read books together.
5. Play hide-and-seek (or, for younger children, peek-a-boo).
6. Play in the sandbox together.
7. Surprise Mom with a special gift: Clean the house, make dinner, or simply make a card expressing your love for her.
8. Sit on the floor with the Legos or Tinker Toys or . . .
9. Go to the park.
10. Ask to pet the dog that your neighbor is walking by.
11. Take your daughter—or son—to work.
12. Go to a ball game together.
13. Play a game of sock wars. Bundled socks are cheap, don't hurt, and usually can't break much around the house.
14. Get the board games out often: Candyland, Yahtzee, LIFE, Monopoly.
15. Let your child use the camera to make a home movie.
16. Take a hike.
17. Play dress-up.
18. Have tea together.
19. Take a day trip to the museum, skiing, or to an indoor playground.
20. Run some errands together.
21. Color together.

22. Make a surprise run to the ice cream shop.
23. Cuddle.
24. Take the dog for a walk.
25. Write your child a note of love and encouragement.
26. Put a picture of the two of you near her bed as a reminder of your love.
27. Say "I love you" every time you think of it.
28. Forgive offenses quickly.
29. Demonstrate grace and mercy.
30. Have a tickle fight.
31. Build a blanket fort and have some snacks.

In Closing

In the New Testament, the apostle Peter wrote about the Old Testament prophets who, like parents, really didn't know how everything was going to turn out (see 1 Peter 1:10–12). Peter said that the prophets spoke about the grace that would come to the Gentiles—but they did not understand just how God was going to save the world through His Son's death and resurrection. The prophets foretold the coming of a suffering Messiah, and His future glory, but they were unable to distinguish when He would appear as a humble servant, nor could they grasp that His second coming would be as King of the world.

God compelled His prophets to speak of things they could not fully understand. They were to prepare the way for the coming of Christ. They told of realities they could not understand, nor would they live to see. They knew they were appointed for a time, but not privileged to participate in what they spoke about. They would also not live to see how you and I have benefited from God's gift of salvation and how we are living our lives in light of His grace.

In a sense, parents and prophets are very much alike. We are given a role to prepare the way—and then to step back and let the future generations make something of our work. We may not (and probably won't) see the end product. We cannot control what those who follow us will do, or how they will choose. Yet we strive with everything within us to provide them what they need. We do this, not to serve ourselves, but to serve them. And their children's children.

Here's to work that will last a long, long time . . .

Addendum
Personality Types Inventory
(from *Making Love Last Forever* by Gary Smalley)
How to Take and Score the Inventory

1. For each temperament type, circle the positive traits (in the left column) that sound the most like you—as you are at home. It will probably help to cover the right-hand column as you take the inventory, to help you focus on the positives. Do not score yourself as you behave at work. (If you want to evaluate your "at work" tendencies, take the test again later, with that environment —or any other—in mind.) For now, ignore the right-hand column.
2. For each trait, add the number of circled traits (in the left column) and then double that number. This is your score.
3. To graph your temperament mix, mark your score for each temperament type on the graph with a large dot. If you want, draw a line to connect the dots.

LION Temperament Characteristics

Likes authority . . . .*Too direct or demanding*

Takes charge . . . .*Pushy; can step in front of others*

Determined . . . .*Overbearing*

Confident . . . .*Cocky*

Firm . . . .*Unyielding*

Enterprising . . . .*Takes big risks*

Competitive . . . .*Cold-blooded*

Enjoys challenges . . . .*Avoids relations*

Problem-solver . . . .*Too busy*

Productive . . . .*Overlooks feelings; do it now!*

Bold . . . .*Insensitive*

Purposeful; goal-driven . . . .*Imbalanced; workaholic*

Decision-maker . . . .*Unthoughtful of others' wishes*

Adventurous . . . .*Impulsive*

Strong-willed . . . .*Stubborn*

Independent; self-reliant . . . .*Avoids people and seeking help*

Controlling . . . .*Bossy; overbearing*

Persistent . . . .*Inflexible*

Action-oriented . . . .*Unyielding*

"Let's do it now!"

Lion Score (double the number circled) —————

OTTER Temperament Characteristics

Enthusiastic . . . .*Overbearing*

Takes risks . . . .*Dangerous and foolish*

Visionary . . . .*Daydreamer*

Motivator . . . .*Manipulator*

Energetic . . . .*Impatient*

Very verbal . . . .*Attacks under pressure*

Promoter . . . .*Exaggerates*

Friendly; mixes easily . . . .*Shallow relationships*

Enjoys popularity . . . .*Too showy*
Fun-loving . . . .*Too flippant; not serious*
Likes variety . . . .*Too scattered*
Spontaneous . . . .*Not focused*
Enjoys change . . . .*Lacks follow-through*
Creative; goes for new ideas . . . .*Too unrealistic; avoids details*
Group-oriented . . . .*Bored with "process"*
Optimistic . . . .*Doesn't see details*
Initiator . . . .*Pushy*
Infectious laughter . . . .*Obnoxious*
Inspirational . . . .*Phony*
"Trust me! It'll work out!"
Otter score (double the number circled) —————

GOLDEN RETRIEVER Temperament Characteristics

Sensitive feelings . . . .*Easily hurt*
Loyal . . . .*Misses opportunities*
Calm; even-keeled . . . .*Lacks enthusiasm*
Nondemanding . . . .*Weakling; pushover*
Avoids confrontations . . . .*Misses honest intimacy*
Enjoys routine . . . .*Stays in rut*
Dislikes change . . . .*Not spontaneous*
Warm and relational . . . .*Fewer deep friends*
Gives in . . . .*Codependent*
Accommodating . . . .*Indecisive*
Cautious humor . . . .*Overly cautious*
Adaptable . . . .*Loses identity*
Sympathetic . . . .*Holds on to others' hurts*
Thoughtful . . . .*Can be taken advantage of*
Nurturing . . . .*Ears get smashed*
Patient . . . .*Crowded out by others*
Tolerant . . . .*Weaker convictions*

Good listener .... *Attracted to hurting people*

Peacemaker .... *Holds personal hurts inside*

"Let's keep things the way they are."

Golden retriever score (double the number circled) ————

BEAVER Temperament Characteristics

Reads all instructions .... *Afraid to break rules*

Accurate .... *Too critical*

Consistent .... *Lacks spontaneity*

Controlled .... *Too serious*

Reserved .... *Stuffy*

Predictable .... *Lacks variety*

Practical .... *Not adventurous*

Orderly .... *Rigid*

Factual .... *Picky*

Conscientious .... *Inflexible*

Perfectionistic .... *Controlling*

Discerning .... *Negative on new opportunities*

Detailed .... *Rarely finishes a project*

Analytical .... *Loses overview*

Inquisitive .... *Smothering*

Precise .... *Strict*

Persistent .... *Pushy*

Scheduled .... *Boring*

Sensitive .... *Stubborn*

"How was it done in the past?"

Beaver score (double the number circled) ————

Chart your results on the next page.

CHARTING THE RESULTS

L	O	GR	B

```
40------------------------------------------------------------------40
35------------------------------------------------------------------35
30------------------------------------------------------------------30
25------------------------------------------------------------------25
20------------------------------------------------------------------20
15------------------------------------------------------------------15
10------------------------------------------------------------------10
5--------------------------------------------------------------------5
0--------------------------------------------------------------------0
```

How did you do? Remember this isn't a pass-fail test. This evaluation simply shows your tendencies and traits. As you look at your charted score, you may see a blend of all four categories. That's fine. Or you may see two scores significantly higher than the others. Or you may have one category that's head and shoulders above the other three. No none pattern is "correct."

Now take note of the right-hand column extreme for each of your circled characteristics. This might be how your positive traits are perceived by your family or friends.

Lions are leaders, decisive, bottom line, problem-solvers, not conversational.

Otters are fun-loving, entertainers, net workers, motivators, creative, talkers.

Retrievers are loving, nurturing, loyal, good listeners, encouragers.

Beavers are hard-working, detailed, accurate, focused on quality.

Consciously work to become more aware of your natural tendencies. Go for a healthy balance, tempering any extreme problem area, focus on your strengths and learn to cultivate the strengths of less dominant personality traits.

Some suggestions for each personality type:

Lions: Be softer and more gentle and include others when making decisions.

Otters: Think before you speak, and consider consequences before you act.

Retrievers: Practice saying no and making firm decisions.

Beavers: Learn to relax and don't expect others to do things just like you.

Adapted by permission from *Making Love Last Forever*, by Gary Smalley (Thomas Nelson).

Notes

1. Truett Cathy, *It's Better to Build Boys Than Mend Men* (Decatur, Geo.: Looking Glass Books, 2004), 15.
2. James C. Dobson, *Bringing Up Boys* (Carol Stream, Ill.: Tyndale, 2001).
3. divorceguide.com/usa/divorce-information/divorce-statistics-in-the-usa.html.
4. Josh McDowell, "Evidence of a Changed Life." See precious-testimonies.com/Hope_Encouragement.k-o/McDowwellJ.htm. Josh has told his story in numerous venues; for more about Josh McDowell, see Josh.org.
5. Ken Canfield, "Your Heritage and Your Legacy," National Center for Fathering, April 30, 2007.
6. C. S. Lewis, *The Problem of Pain* (New York: HarperOne, 2001), 31.
7. Michael Gurian and Kathy Stevens, "With Boys and Girls in Mind," *Educational Leadership*, November 2004.
8. Leonard Sax, *Why Gender Matters* (New York: Broadway Books, 2006), 42.
9. Gurian and Stevens, "With Boys and Girls in Mind."
10. Ibid.
11. Ibid.
12. Os Guiness, *The Call* (Nashville, Thomas Nelson, 2003), 162.
13. barna.org/barna-update/article/15-familykids/321-new-research-explores-the-long-term-effect-of-spiritual-activity-among-children-and-teens.
14. James C. Dobson, *Solid Answers* (Carol Stream, Ill.: Tyndale, 1997).
15. Chuck Colson, prisonfellowship.org/PrisonFellowship/ChannelRoot/Issues/ColsonsPerspective/Remove+the+Blinders.htm.

Acknowledgments

It is a great privilege to be surrounded in life by so many terrific, supportive, encouraging relatives, friends, and associates (Proverbs 11:14). I'm grateful to the following, who played a part in the formation of this book:

Sean, for asking how to be a good dad. Your heart for your daughter moved me and eventually prompted this book. Although we've lost touch, I pray the two of you are close.

My brother Mike Fuller, for offering wise advice that day in the park to the young man who admitted he didn't quite know how to be a good dad.

Dan Eickmeier, Ron Flynn, and the others who have been part of The GWH. We've hiked countless miles in the Rockies, searching for elk, enjoying exciting adventures, sharing laughter, and exchanging parenting insights.

Dr. James C. Dobson, for your coaching, affirmation, and encouragement over the years.

Robert Wolgemuth, for asking, "Is there a book inside you?"

Erik Wolgemuth for being a champion and a trusted guide through the publishing process.

The team at Moody Publishers for your expertise and enthusiasm for this project.

John Peckham, for your ongoing friendship and prayers. And for suggesting book ideas that day we drove up to see the Rockies.

My assistant Pat Dahlberg for your help in making the calendar work, and for your ongoing interest in and prayers for my family.

Eric and the great folks at Umpire Estate Mountain Roasters for the incredible coffee and inviting place to write.

Friends who have offered endorsements. I'm grateful for your kindness and enthusiasm!

Through the years I've benefitted incredibly from countless other men who offered advice, anecdotes, and assurances that I could be a good dad. You've shared with me, listened to me, prayed with and for me. There are too many of you to list here! I offer my humble and sincere thanks for your investment in my life, and trust this book will serve in some small way to continue your legacy of impact in the lives of many, many new fathers.

THE HEART OF A FATHER

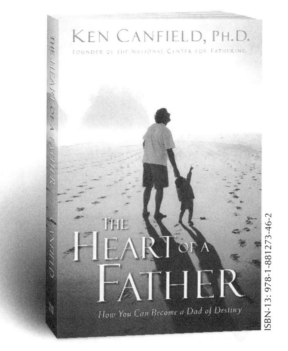

ISBN-13: 978-1-881273-46-2

Every father has a hidden longing to see his children surpass him. To help him achieve this, Ken Canfield offers a three-part plan: examining one's heart, connecting with children, and planning for a lifetime of involved fathering. Canfield also explores how a father should resolve his relationship with his own father. Finally, he explains how to build the four "walls" or dimensions of fathering: involvement, awareness, consistency, and nurturing.

From being a new father to being a grandfather, dads face challenges at each stage of their life. With the long-range perspective this book provides, fathers can anticipate and prepare for the changing situations they'll face. Based on years of careful research involving thousands of fathers, this book is a solid reference tool for dads.

MOODY
PUBLISHERS

moodypublishers.com

THE FIVE LOVE LANGUAGES OF CHILDREN

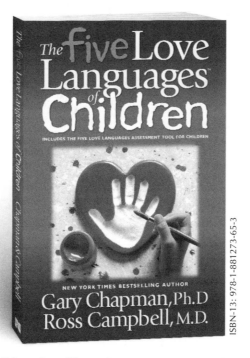

ISBN-13: 978-1-881273-65-3

Does your child speak a different language? Sometimes they fight for your attention, and other times they ignore you completely. Sometimes they are filled with gratitude and affection, and other times they seem totally indifferent. Attitude. Behavior. Development. Everything depends on the love relationship between you and your child. When children feel loved, they do their best. But how can you make sure your child feels loved?

Discover your child's primary love language and learn what you can do to effectively convey unconditional feelings of respect, affection, and commitment that will resonate in your child's emotions and behavior.

MOODY
PUBLISHERS

moodypublishers.com

FOR MARRIED MEN ONLY

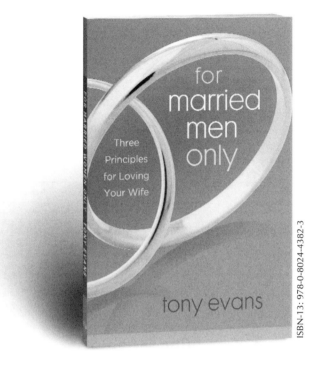

ISBN-13: 978-0-8024-4382-3

What does it mean for a husband to love his wife? Three things, says Tony Evans: a husband must be his wife's savior, sanctifier, and satisfier. It is by living out these three principles that a godly marriage will blossom and flourish.

In *For Married Men Only*, each of these principles is explored and explained using real-life examples. How can a husband be his wife's savior? By learning to love her as Christ loved the church. What about sanctifier? By dying to self and modeling sacrificial love, no matter what the result. And satisfier? By studying and serving his wife so he can fulfill her needs, just as Christ humbled Himself for our sakes.

MOODY
PUBLISHERS

moodypublishers.com

START YOUR FAMILY

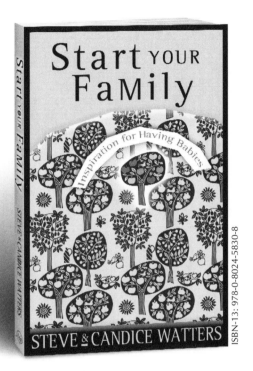

ISBN-13: 978-0-8024-5830-8

In *Start Your Family,* Steve and Candice Watters encourage couples to be intentional about their timeline in the early years of marriage and trust God to help them boldly launch their families. Responding to the most common doubts and hurdles, they offer biblical inspiration for the questions, "Why have kids?," "When is the best time to start?," and "How can we fit kids into our lives?"

MOODY
PUBLISHERS

moodypublishers.com